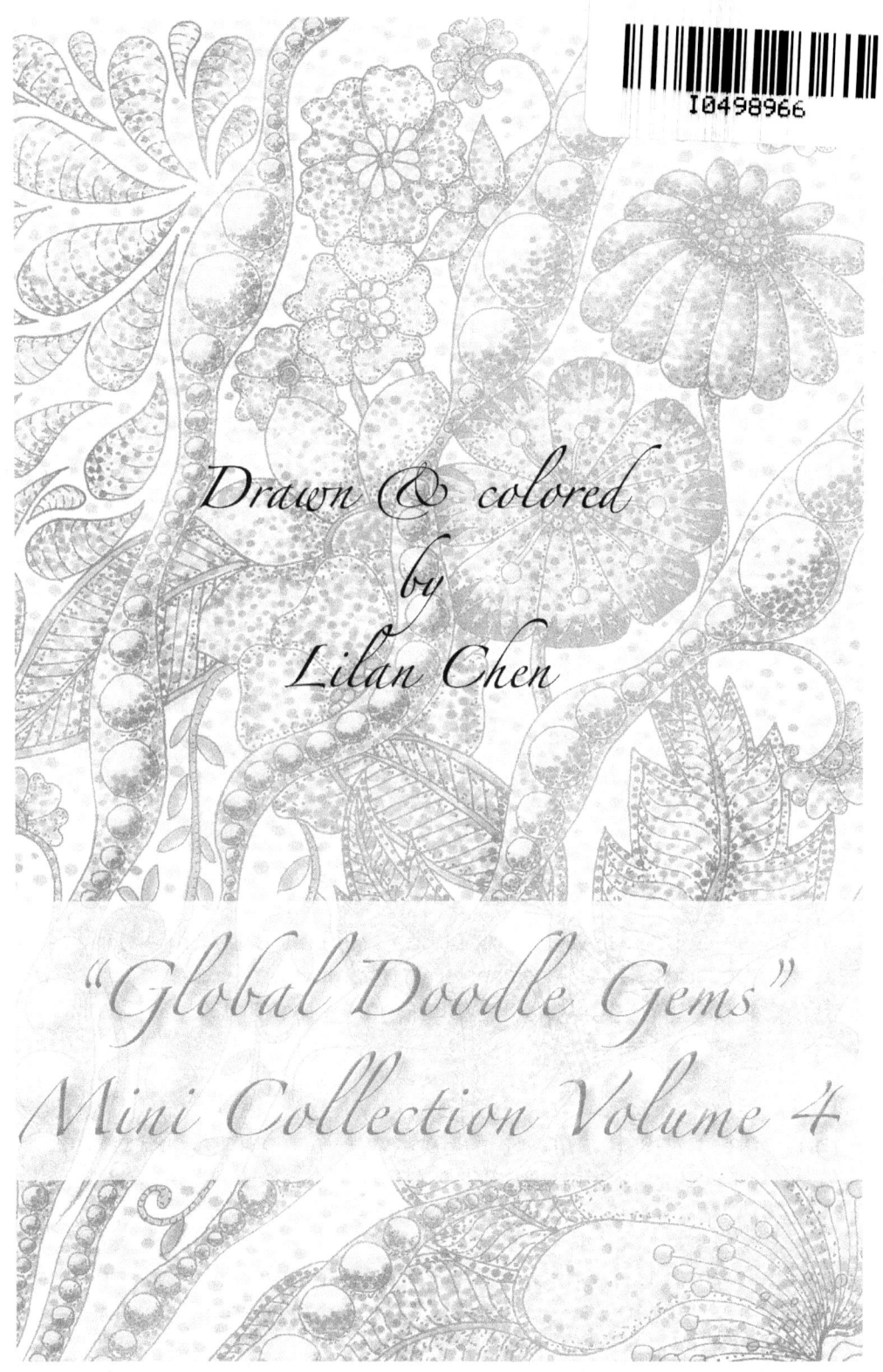

Drawn & colored
by
Lilan Chen

"Global Doodle Gems"
Mini Collection Volume 4

Share your colored versions with us !

The Official FB book page, stay on top of what we have in the works !
www.facebook.com/globaldoodlegems

The Community group, share your colored pages, meet the artists, enjoy exclusive freebies, take part in community Charity books and so much more......
www.facebook.com/groups/globaldoodlegems/

Follow us on Twitter.... @GlobalDoodlegem

We are on Instagram too
@globaldoodlegems for instagram

...and if you are not social like that we have a blog
globaldoodlegems.wordpress.com

Copyright © 2015 Global Doodle Gems
Published by Global Doodle Gems
Anna-Marie Vibeke Wedel

All rights are reserved by Global Doodle Gems.

Duplication of pages for personal use are allowed. You are invited to color the pages then scan/post your coloured versions to social networks, mentioning the book title and author/artist
(Global Doodle Gems).

All artwork and images are protected by copyright laws. This book or any portion thereof may not, otherwise, be reproduced and/or distributed or transmitted without the express written permission of the artist/publisher of Global Doodle Gems.

All of us from the Global Doodle Gems wish you a colortastic time and look forward to seeing your wonderful color results online !

Published by
"GDG"
Global Doodle Gems

Contributing Artists
"Global Doodle Gems"
Mini Collection Volume 4
Thank you for your contributions

Alfred E. Villanueva, Arianne Schimmel, Audrey Sagh, Gemeta Ling, Johanna Ans, Lilan Chen, Lynne McGee, T.J., Marieke Raterman-Bos, Ellen Wolters, Mireille W., Nancy43, Peggy Sue's Artwork, Rover Hsiao, Velvet Comeau
&
Diana Holmes

Contributing Artist
Alfred E. Villanueva
Philippines
Facebook : viworksart2015

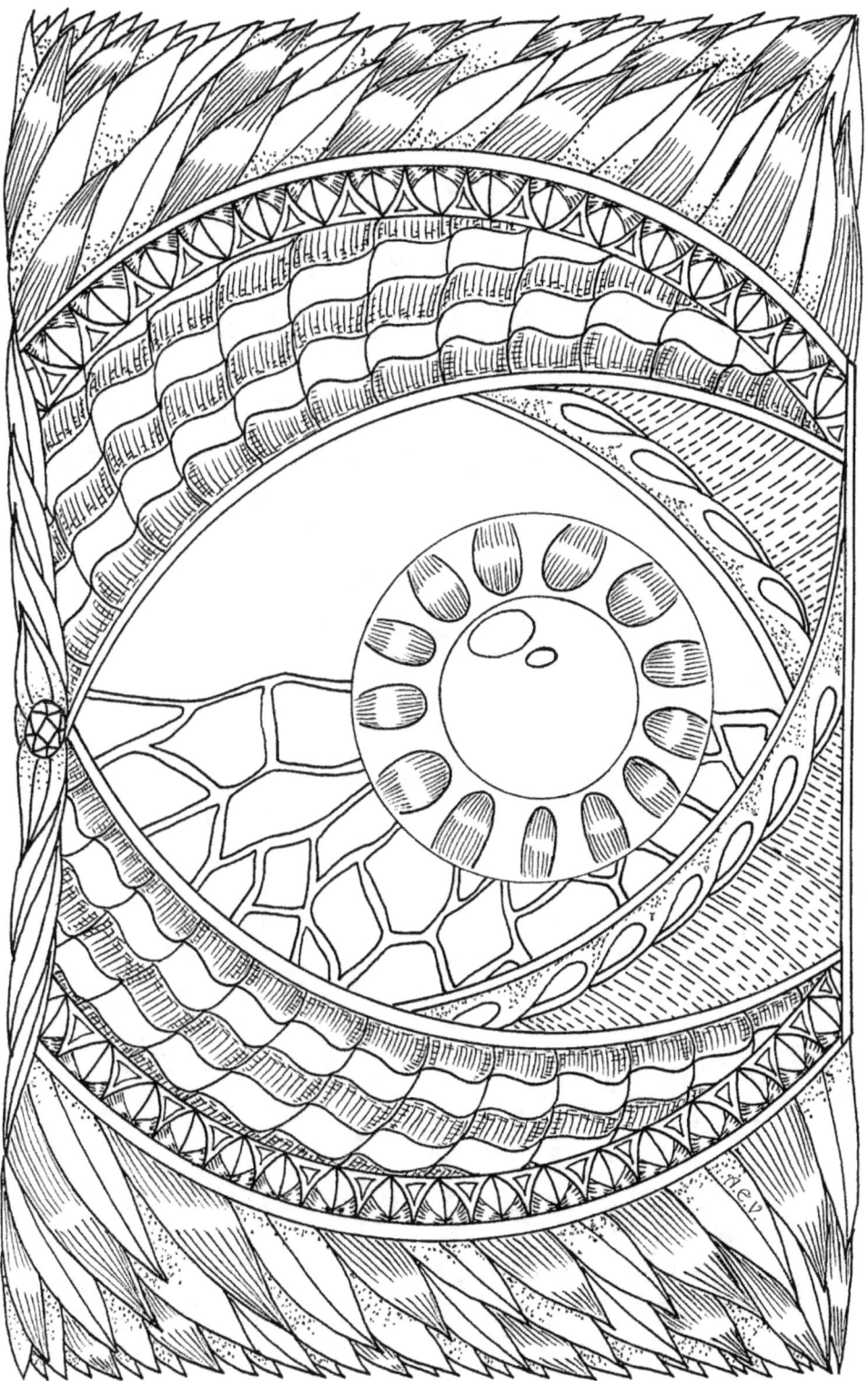

Contributing Artist
Alfred E. Villanueva
Philippines
Facebook : viworksart2015

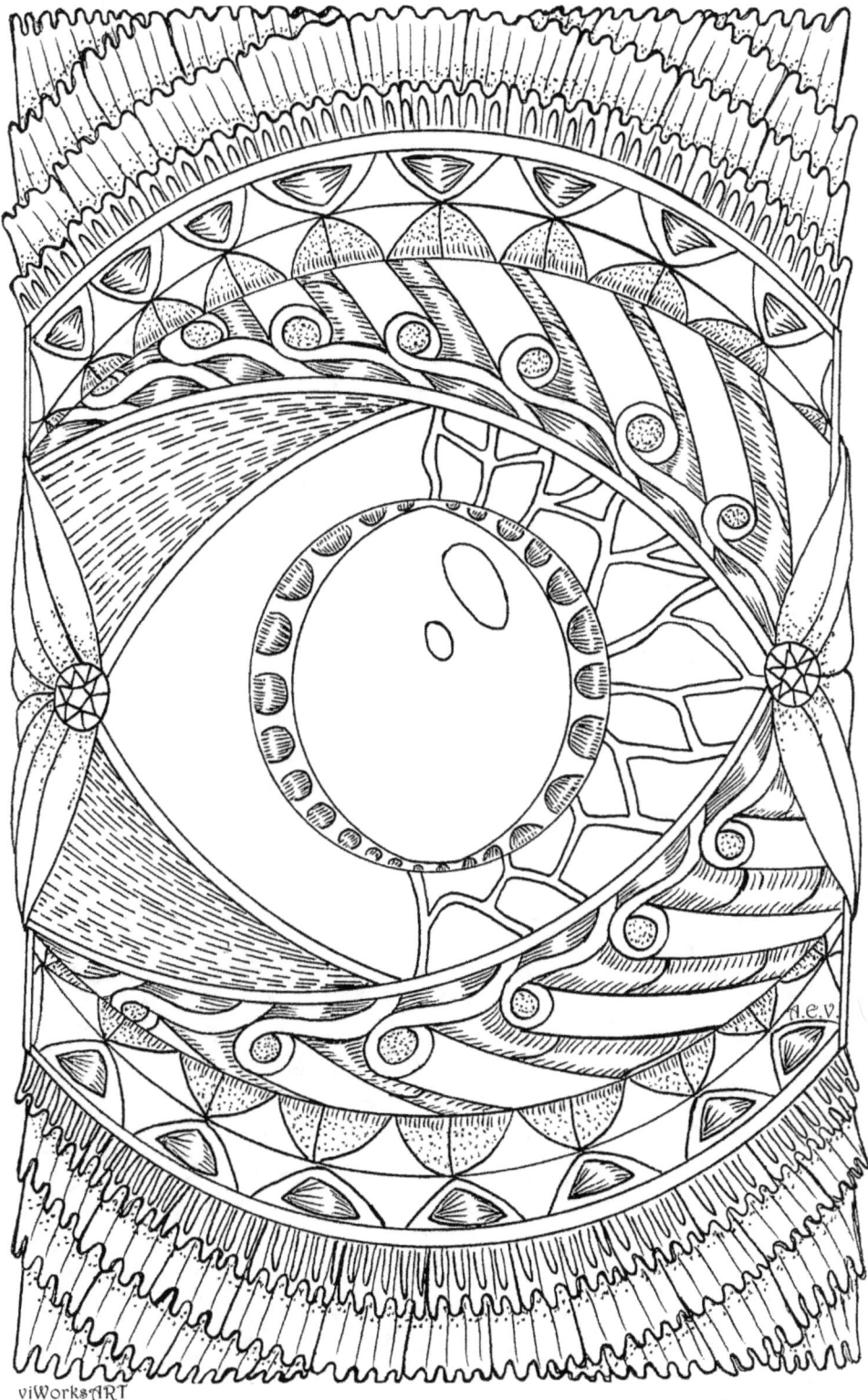

Contributing Artist
Alfred E. Villanueva
Philippines
Facebook : viworksart2015

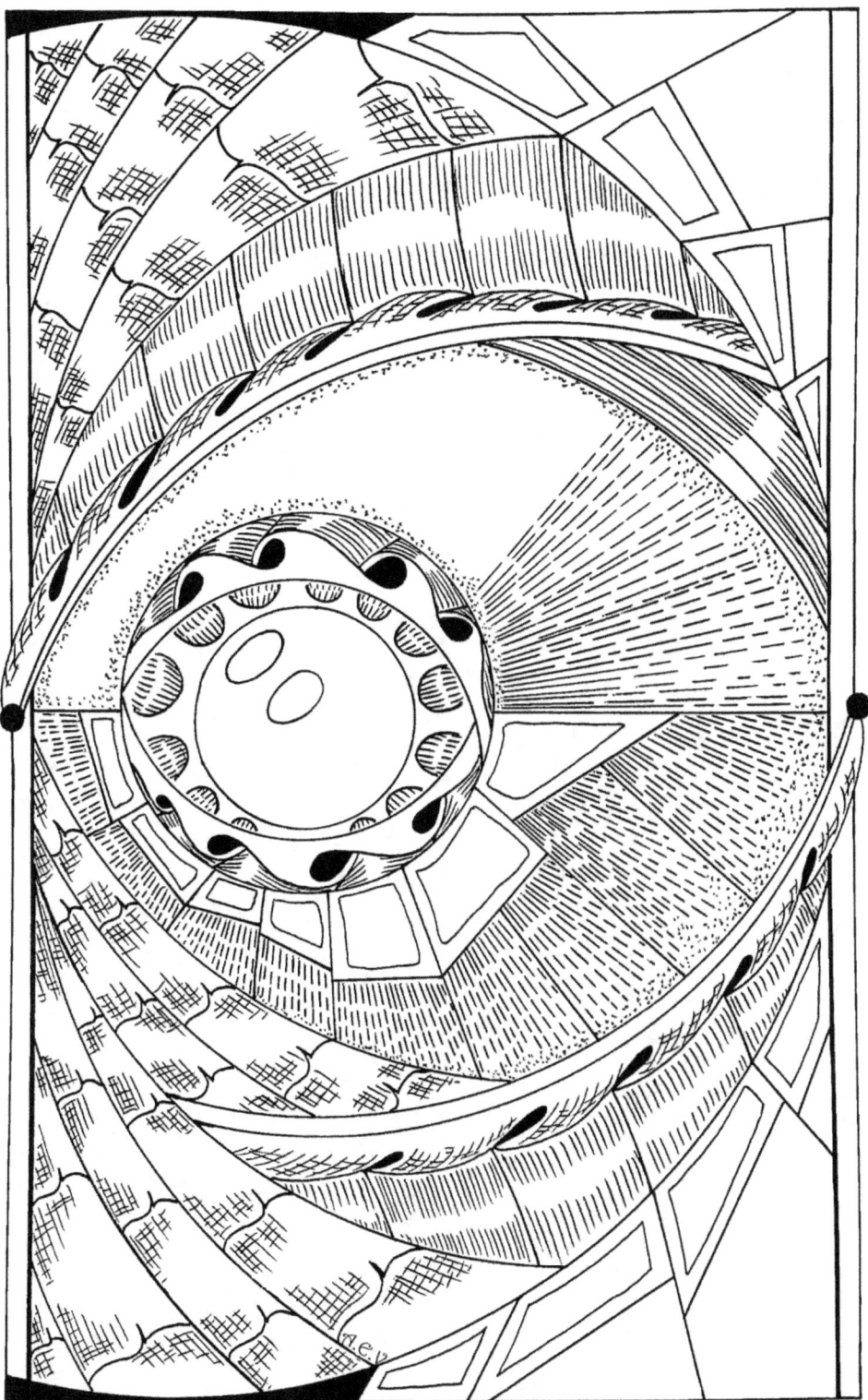

Contributing Artist
Alfred E. Villanueva
Philippines
Facebook : viworksart2015

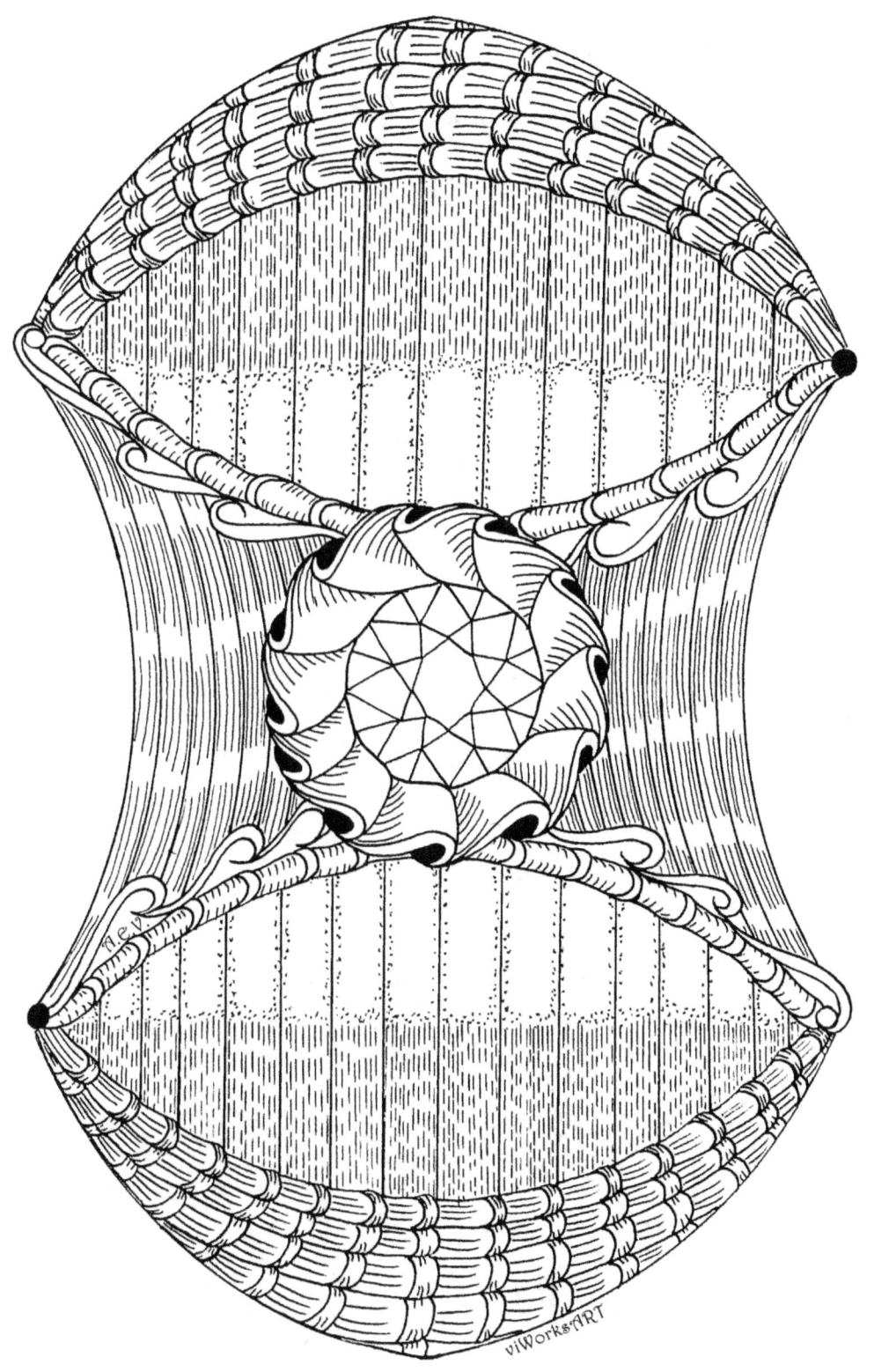

Contributing Artist
Alfred E. Villanueva
Philippines
Facebook : viworksart2015

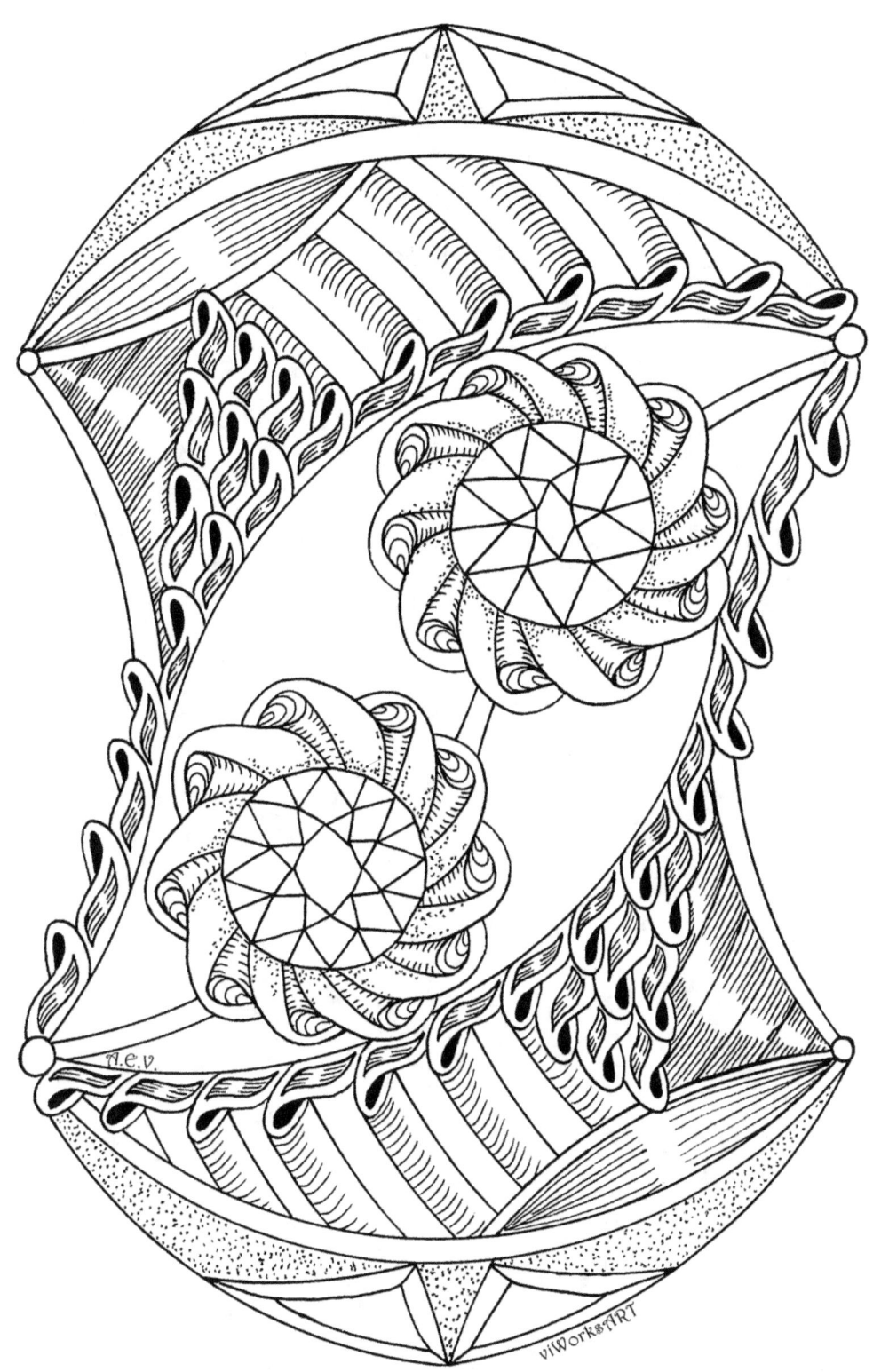

Contributing Artist
Alfred E. Villanueva
Philippines

Facebook : viworksart2015

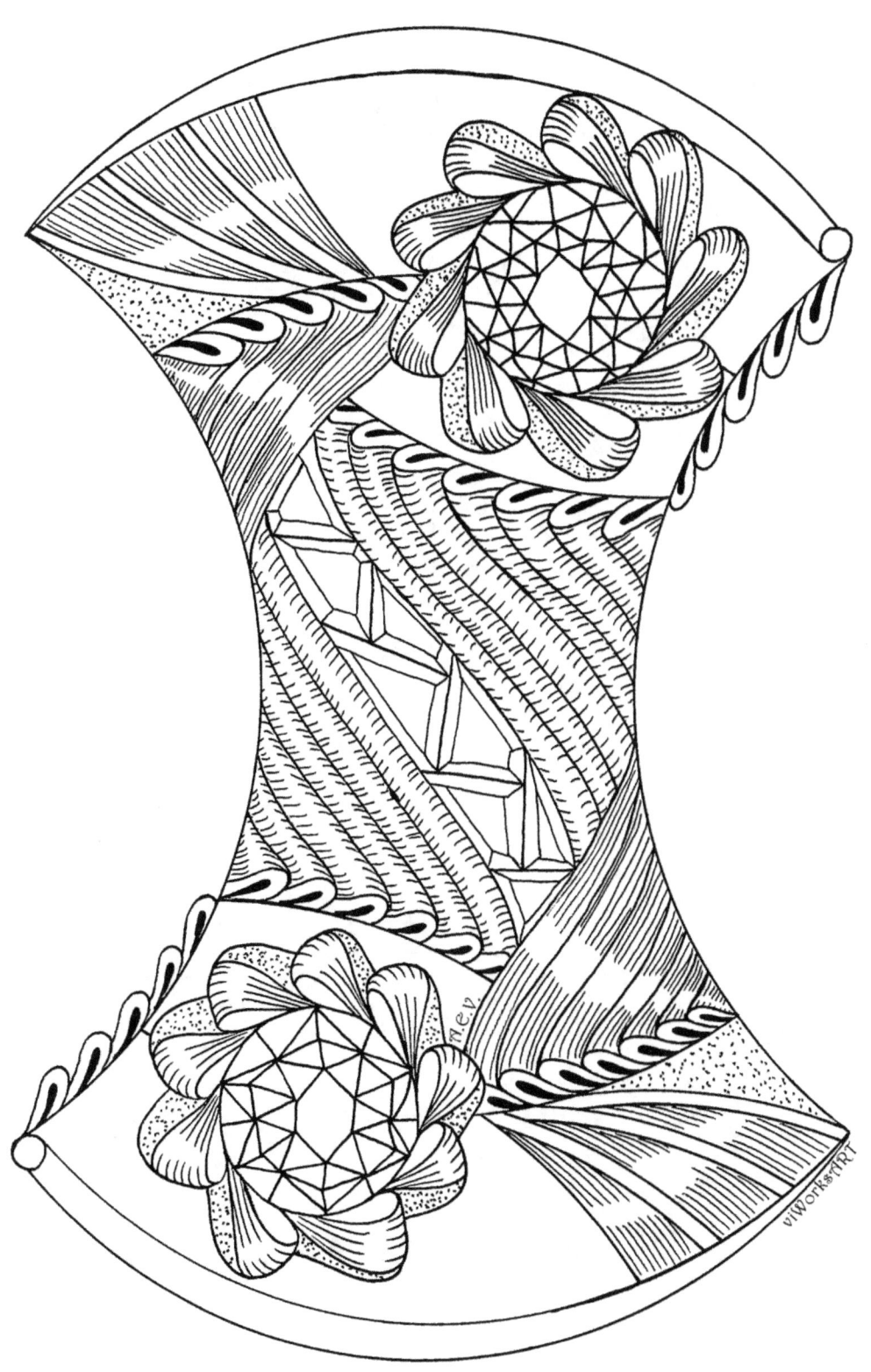

*Contributing Artist
АrianneS Artwork
The Netherlands*

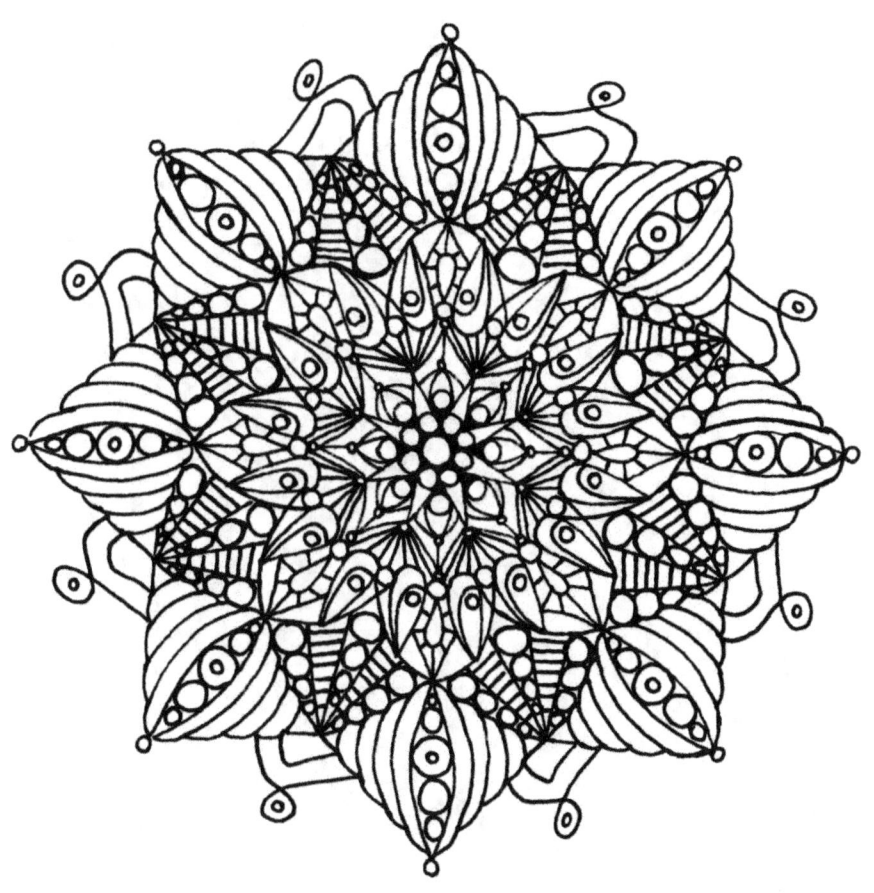

*Contributing Artist
ArianneS Artwork
The Netherlands*

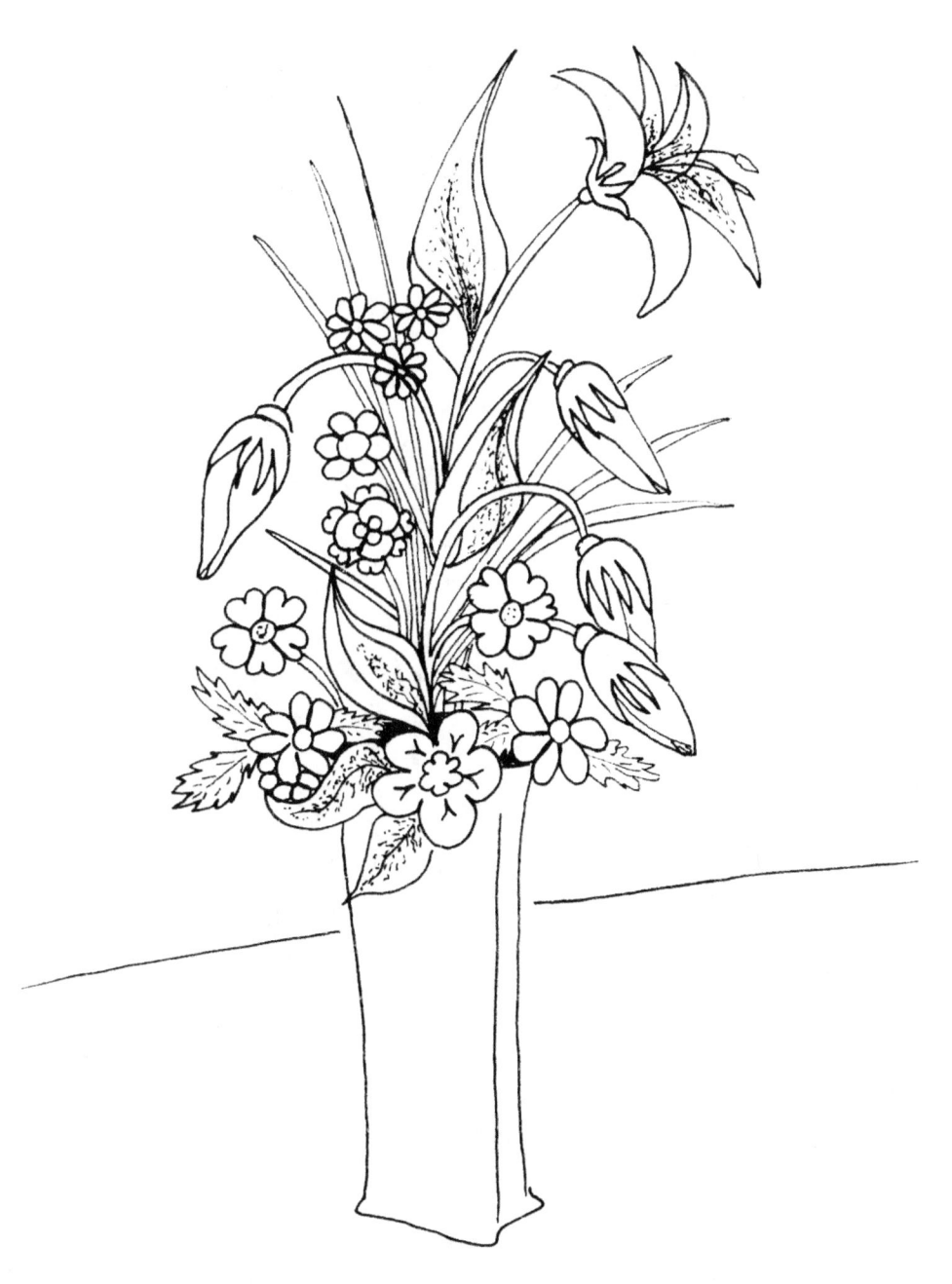

Contributing Artist
Audrey Sagh
Saskatoon, Saskatchewan Canada

Facebook : AMS-Artwork

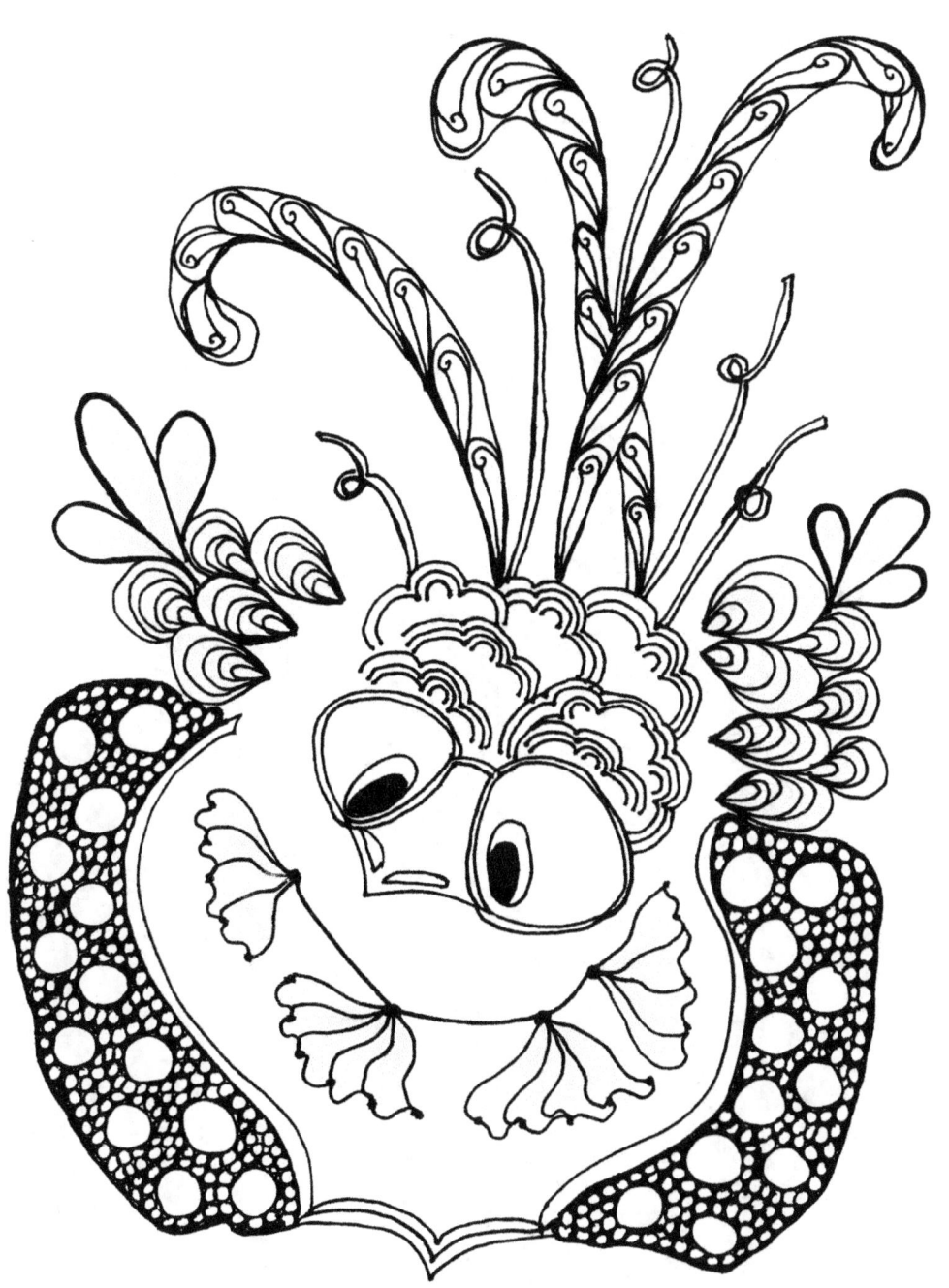

Contributing Artist
Audrey Sagh
Saskatoon, Saskatchewan Canada

Facebook : AMS-Artwork

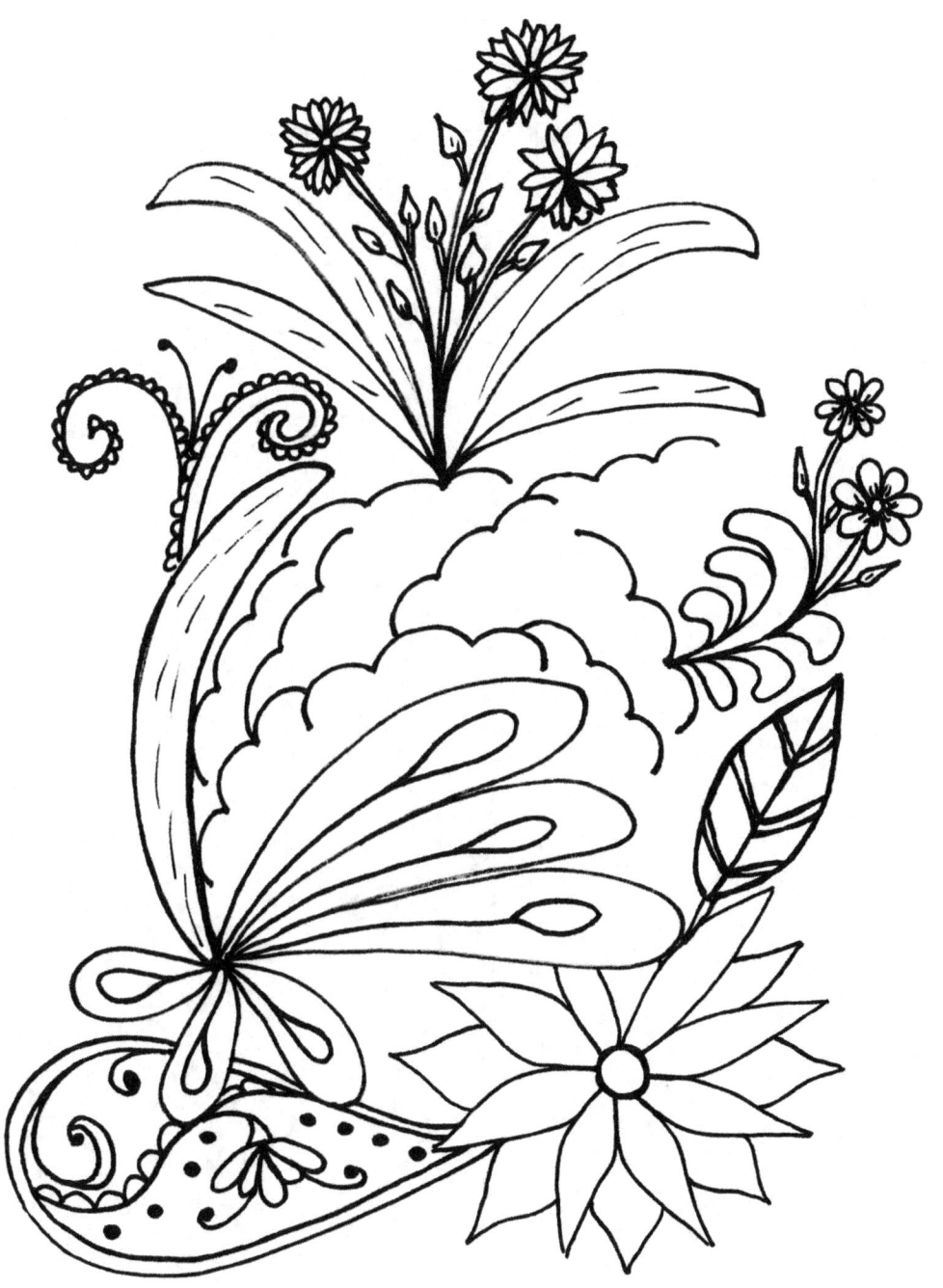

Contributing Artist
Audrey Sagh
Saskatoon, Saskatchewan Canada

Facebook : AMS-Artwork

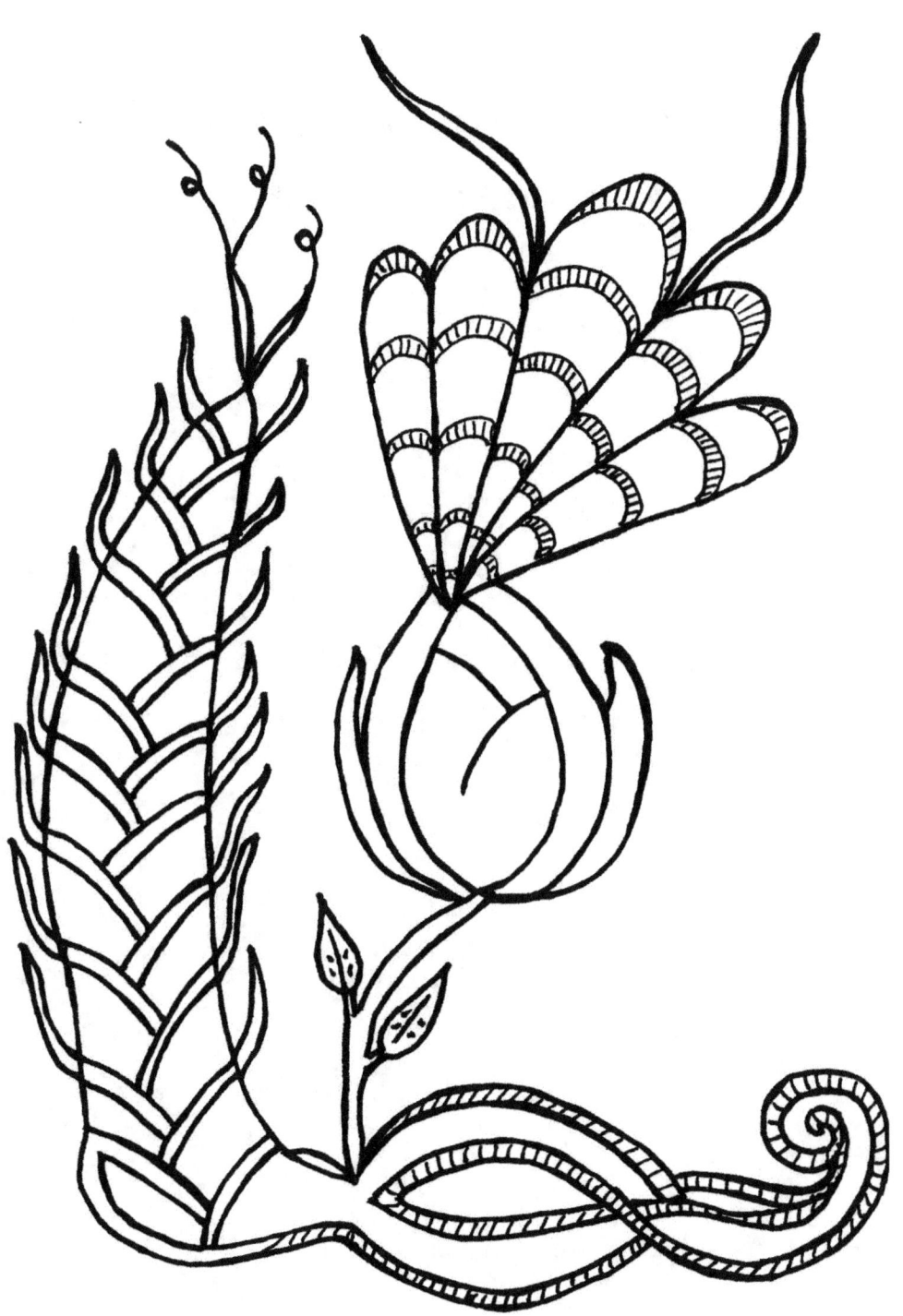

Contributing Artist
Audrey Sagh
Saskatoon, Saskatchewan Canada

Facebook : AMS-Artwork

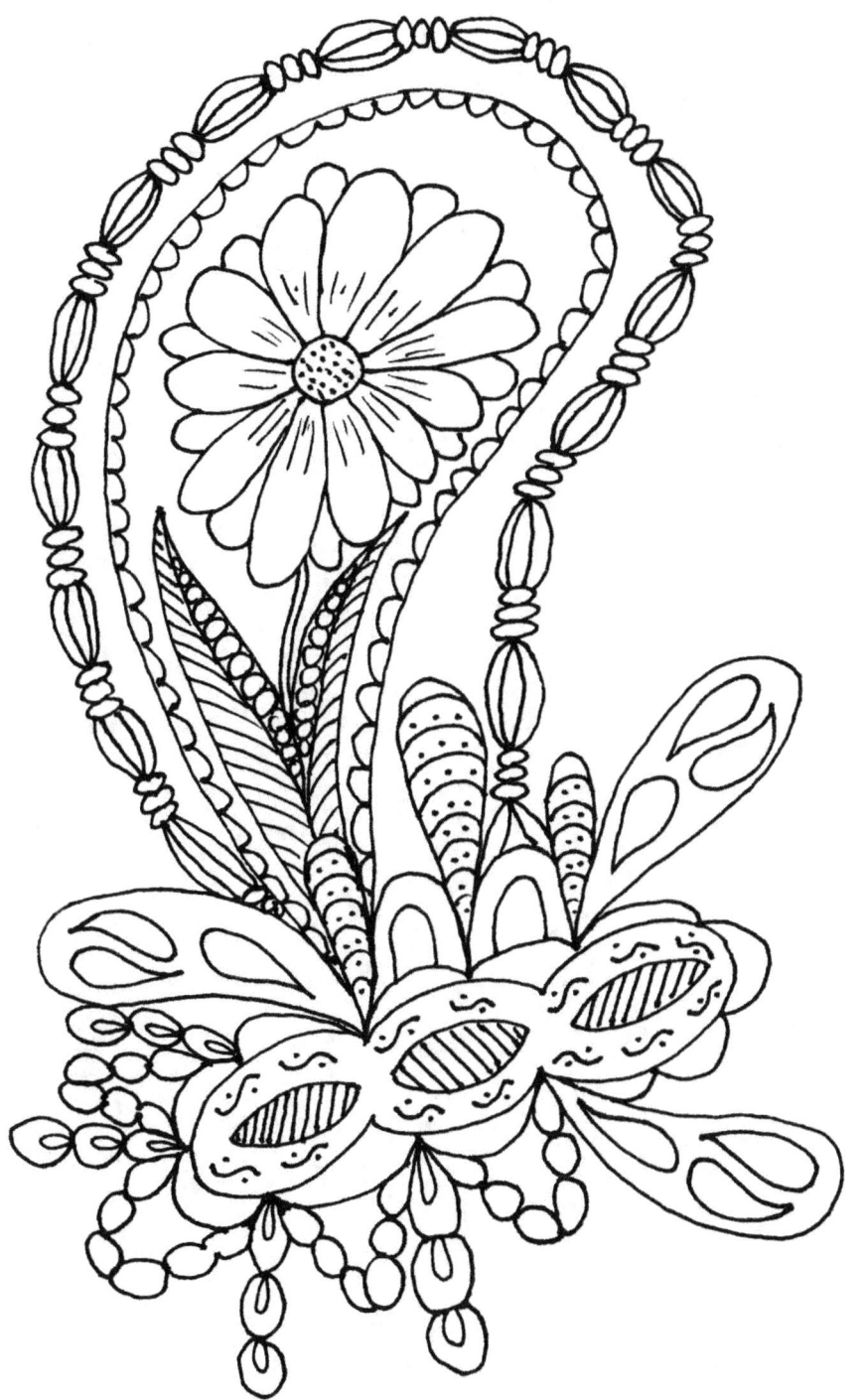

Contributing Artist
Audrey Sagh
Saskatoon, Saskatchewan Canada

Facebook : AMS-Artwork

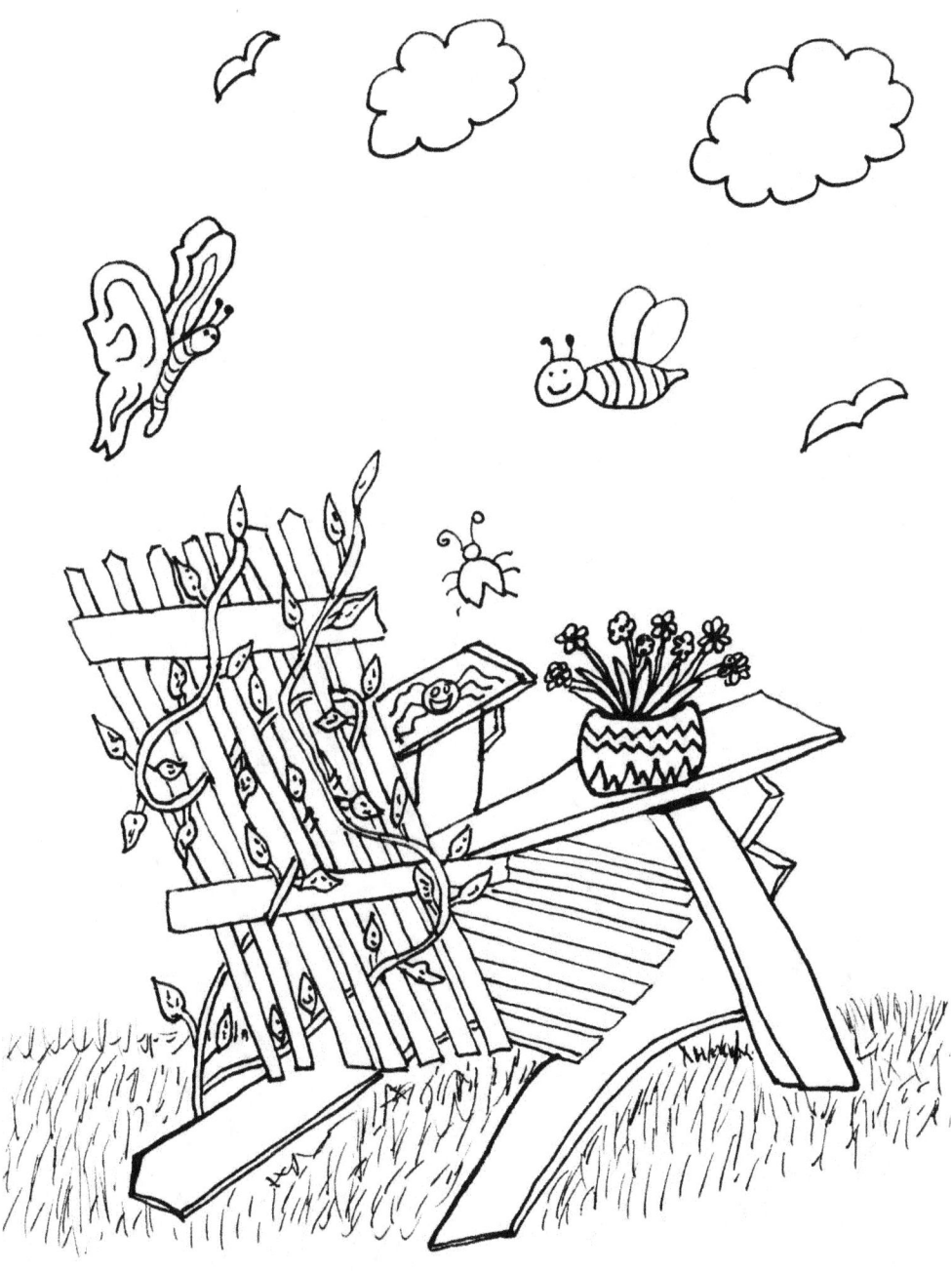

Contributing Artist
Gemeta Ling
Germany

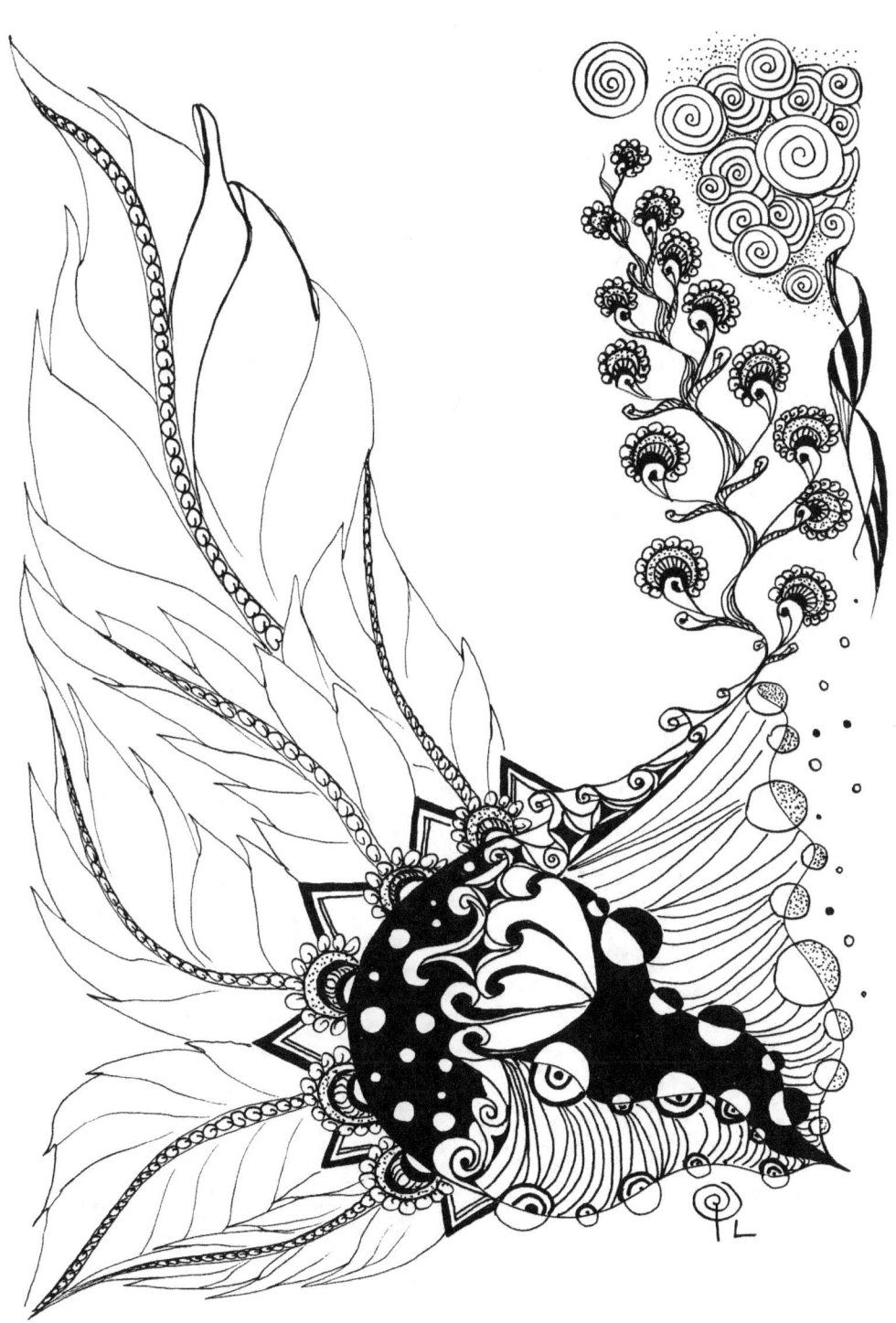

Contributing Artist
Gemeta Ling
Germany

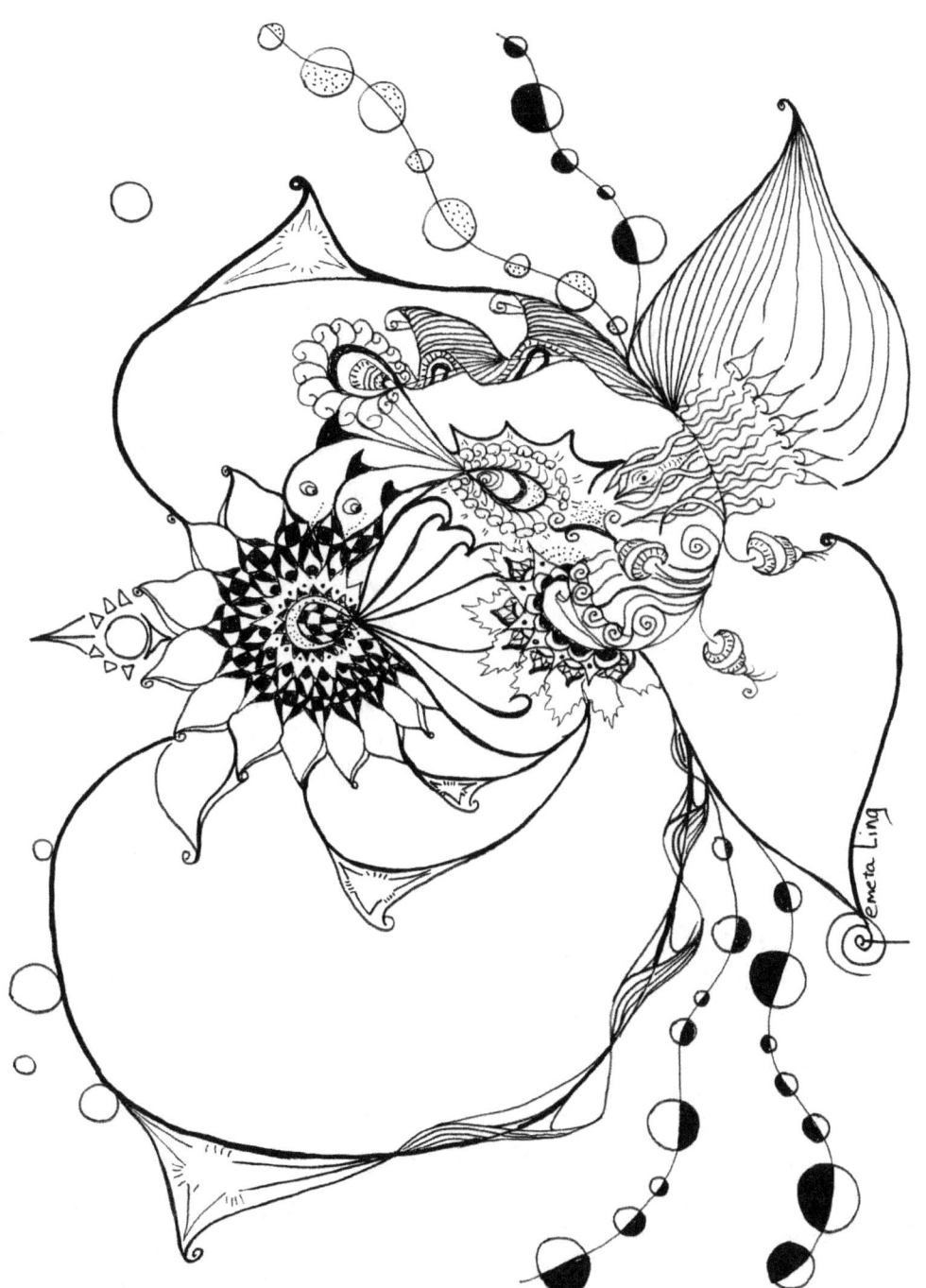

Contributing Artist
Gemeta Ling
Germany

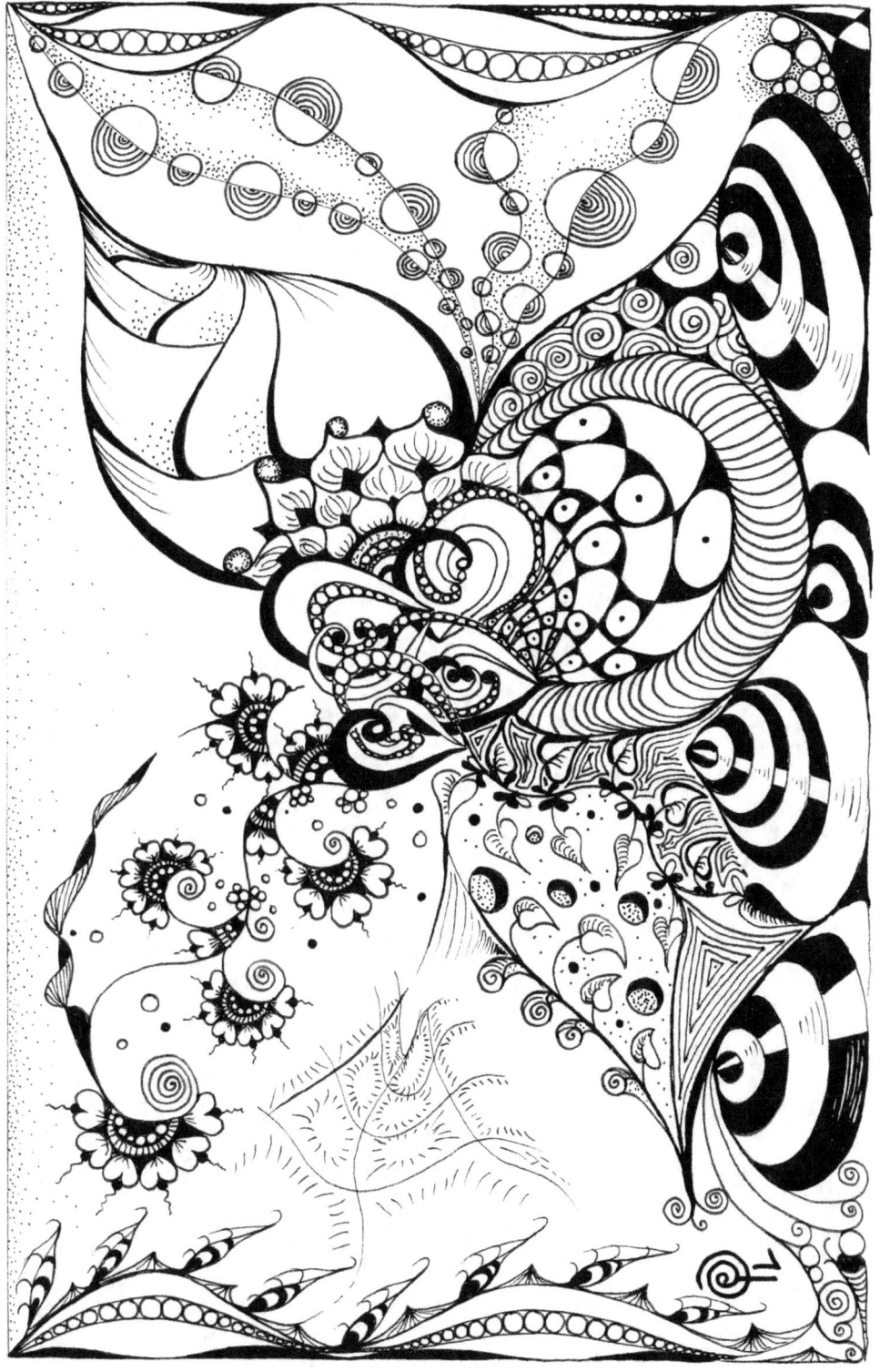

Contributing Artist
MWMS-Johanna Ans
The Netherlands

Blog : mywaymystylejohannaans.wordpress.com

Facebook : Johanna-Ans-My-creative-site

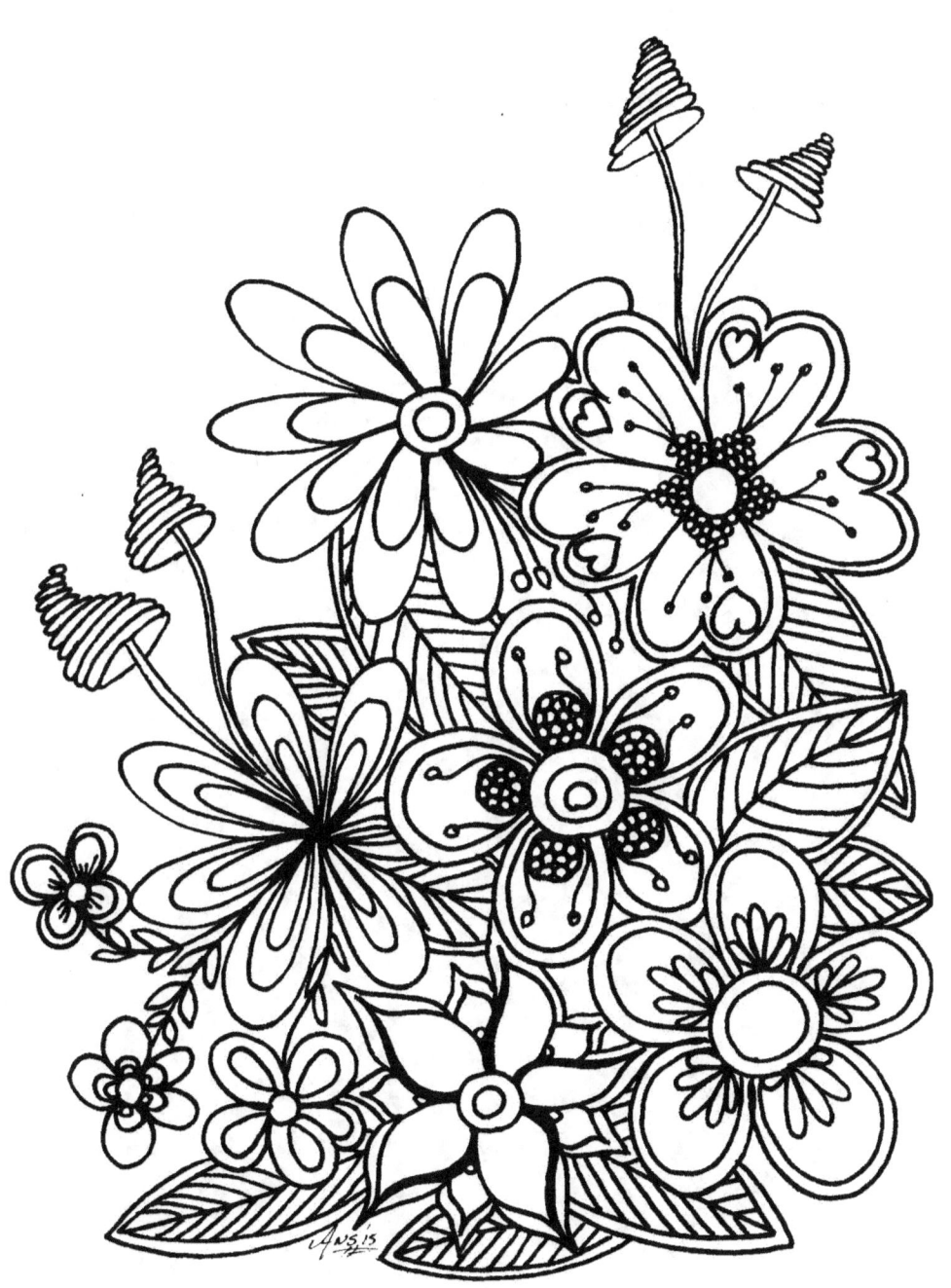

Contributing Artist
MWMS-Johanna Ans
The Netherlands

Blog : mywaymystylejohannaans.wordpress.com

Facebook : Johanna-Ans-My-creative-site

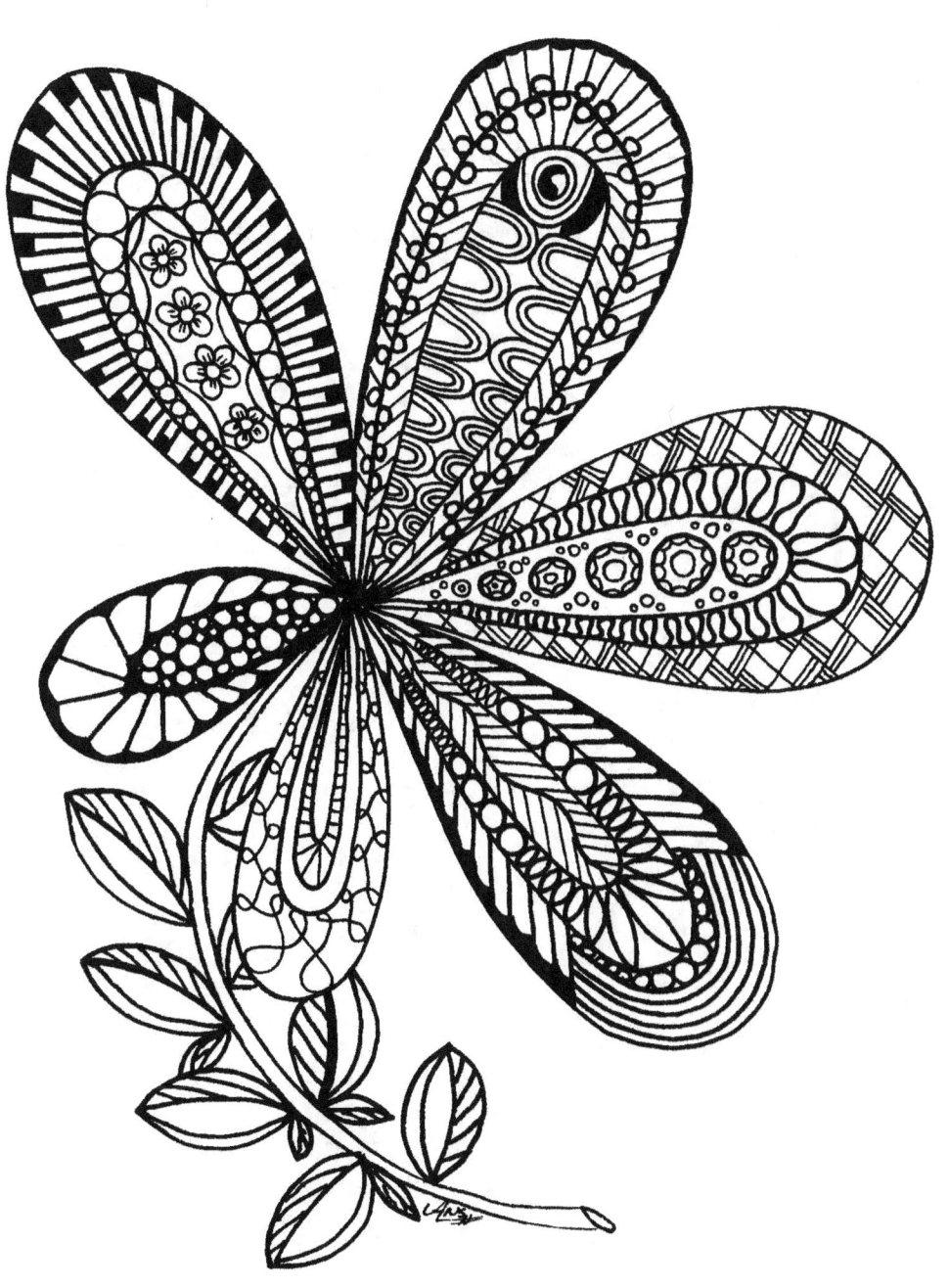

Contributing Artist
MWMS-Johanna Ans
The Netherlands

Blog : mywaymystylejohannaans.wordpress.com

Facebook : Johanna-Ans-My-creative-site

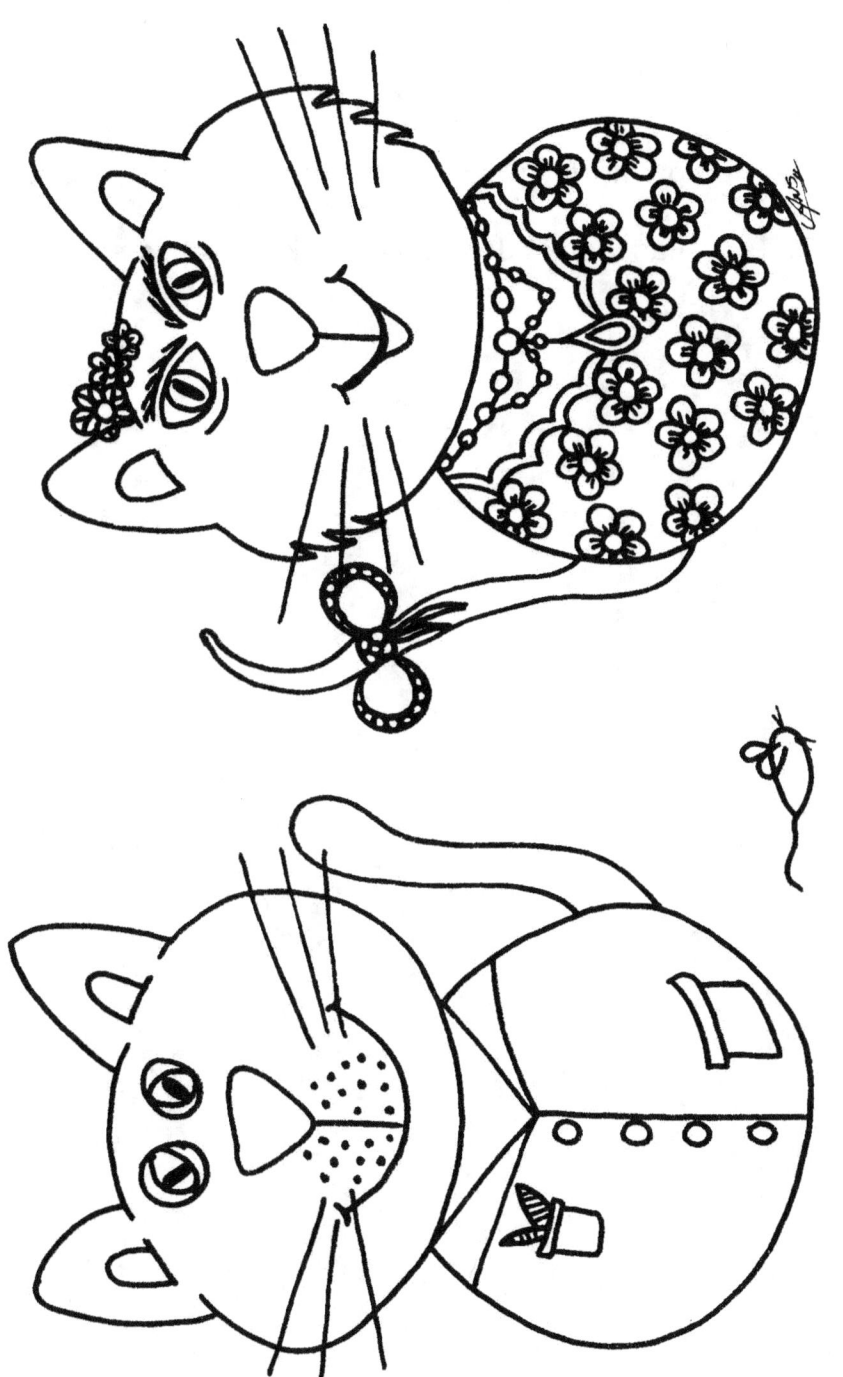

Contributing Artist
MWMS-Johanna Ans
The Netherlands

Blog : mywaymystylejohannaans.wordpress.com

Facebook : Johanna-Ans-My-creative-site

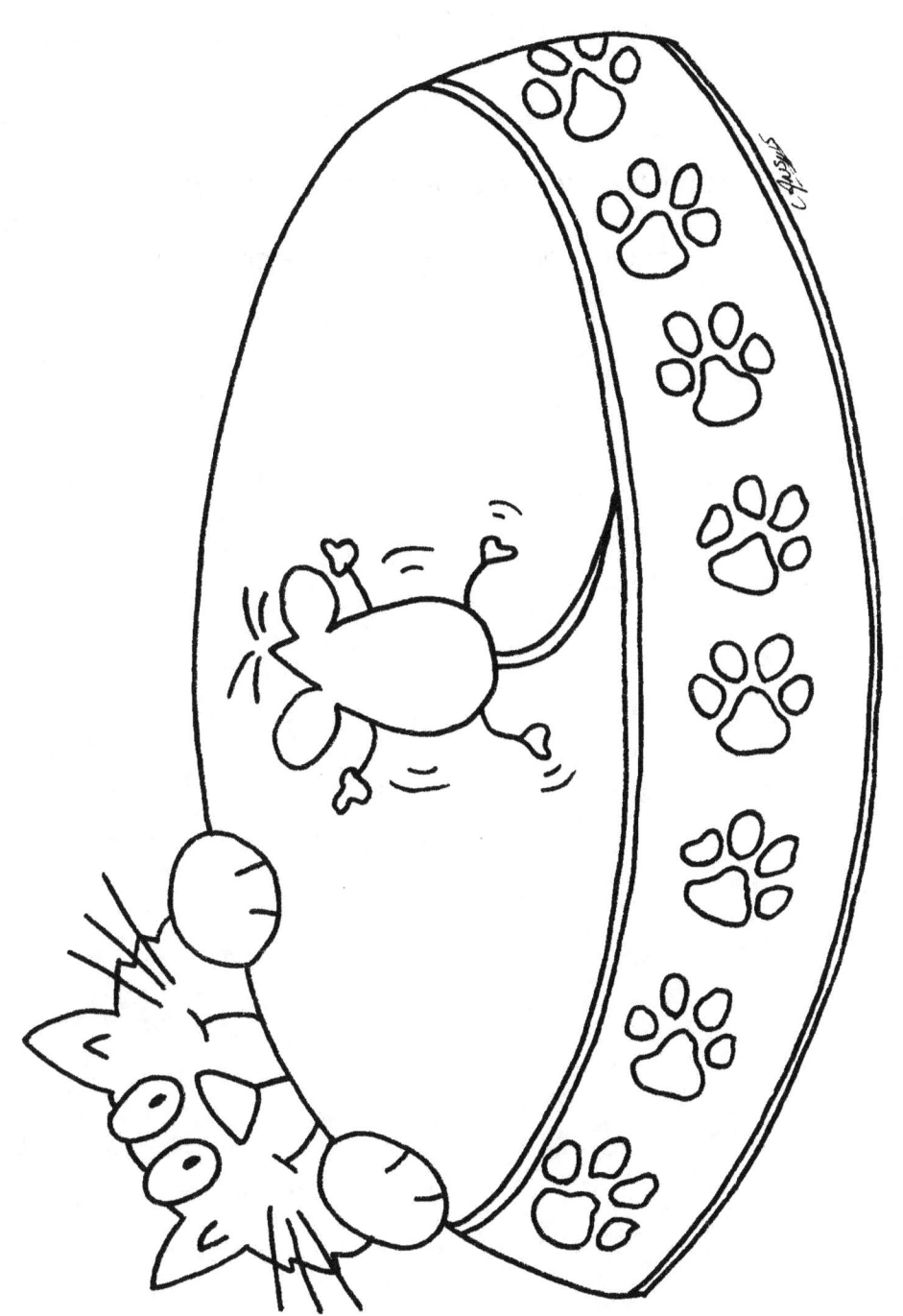

Contributing Artist
MWMS-Johanna Ans
The Netherlands

Blog : mywaymystylejohannaans.wordpress.com

Facebook : Johanna-Ans-My-creative-site

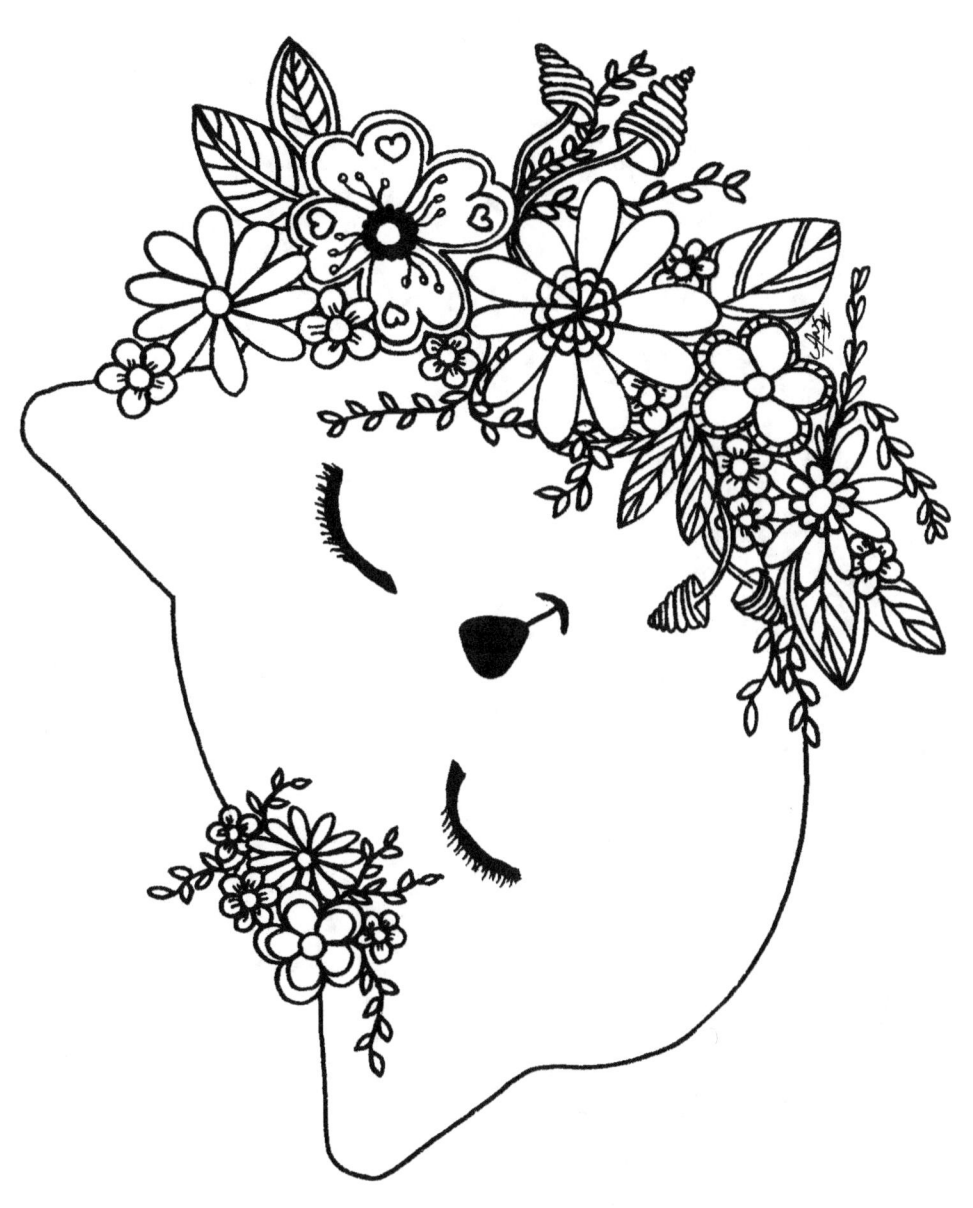

Contributing Artist
Lilan Chen
Taiwan

Facebook : lilanchen.art

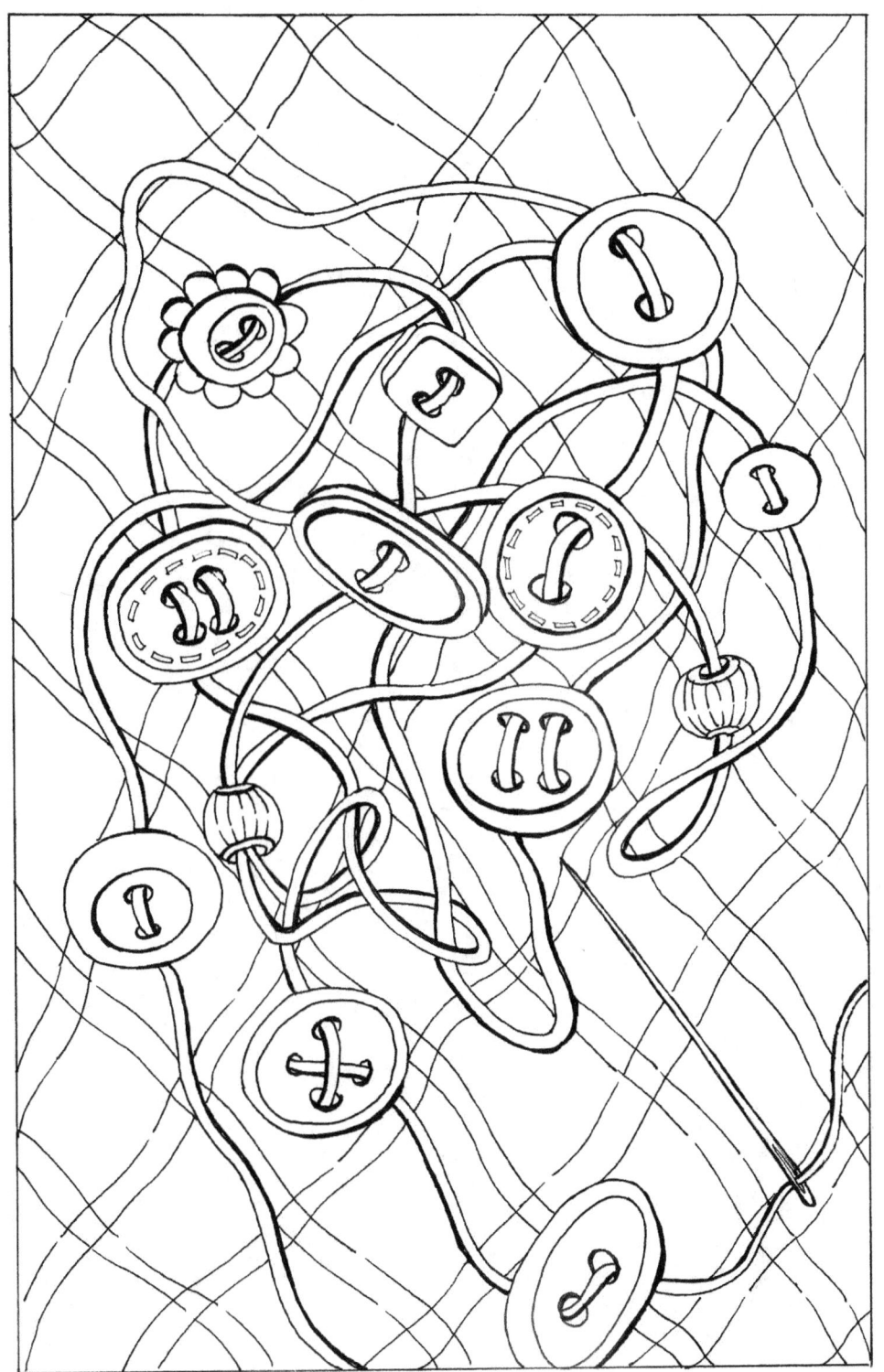

Contributing Artist
Lilan Chen
Taiwan

Facebook : lilanchen.art

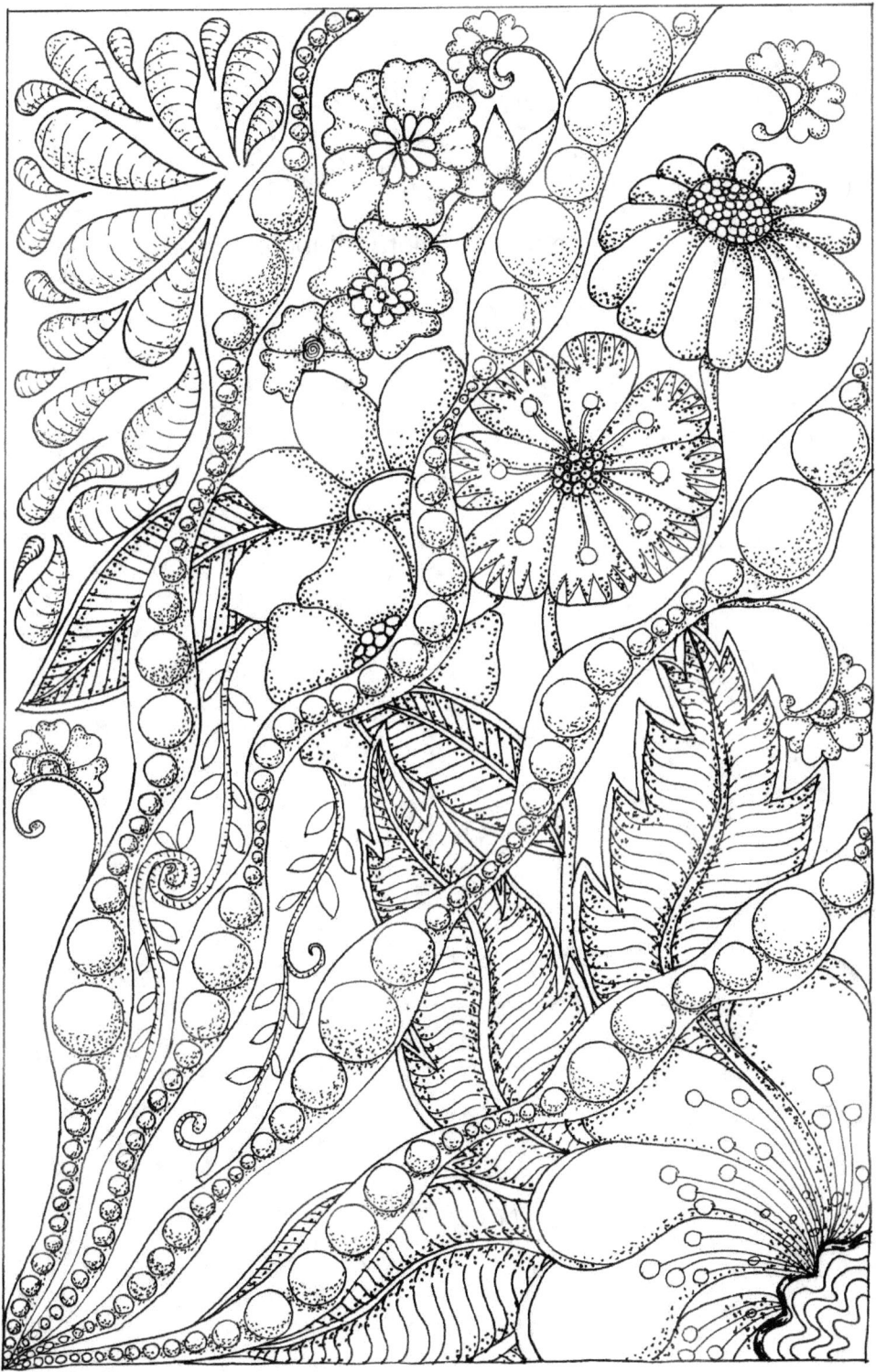

Contributing Artist
Lynne McGee
Brisbane, Australia

Facebook : Colorandtangle

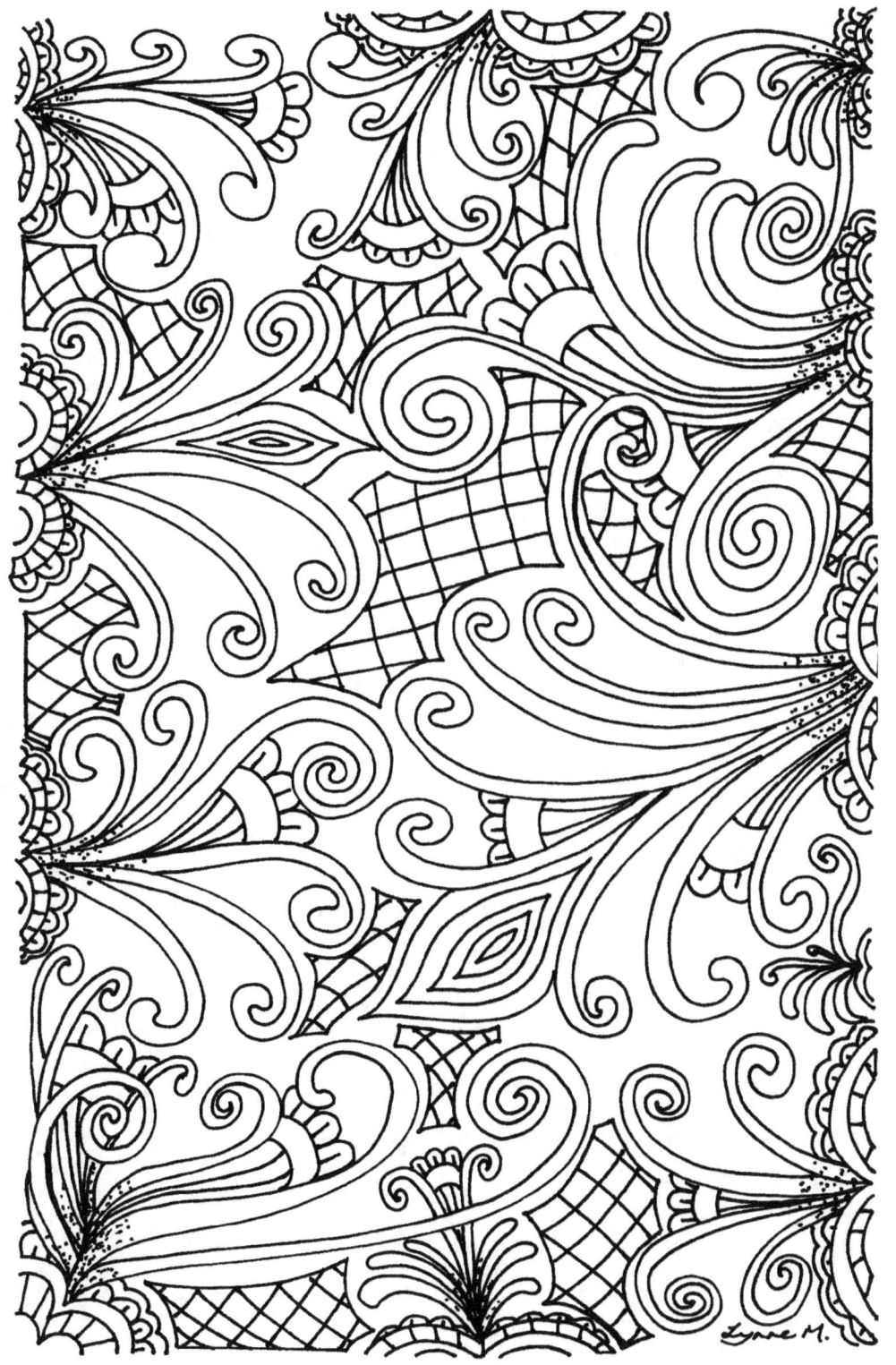

Contributing Artist
Lynne McGee
Brisbane, Australia

Facebook : Colorandtangle

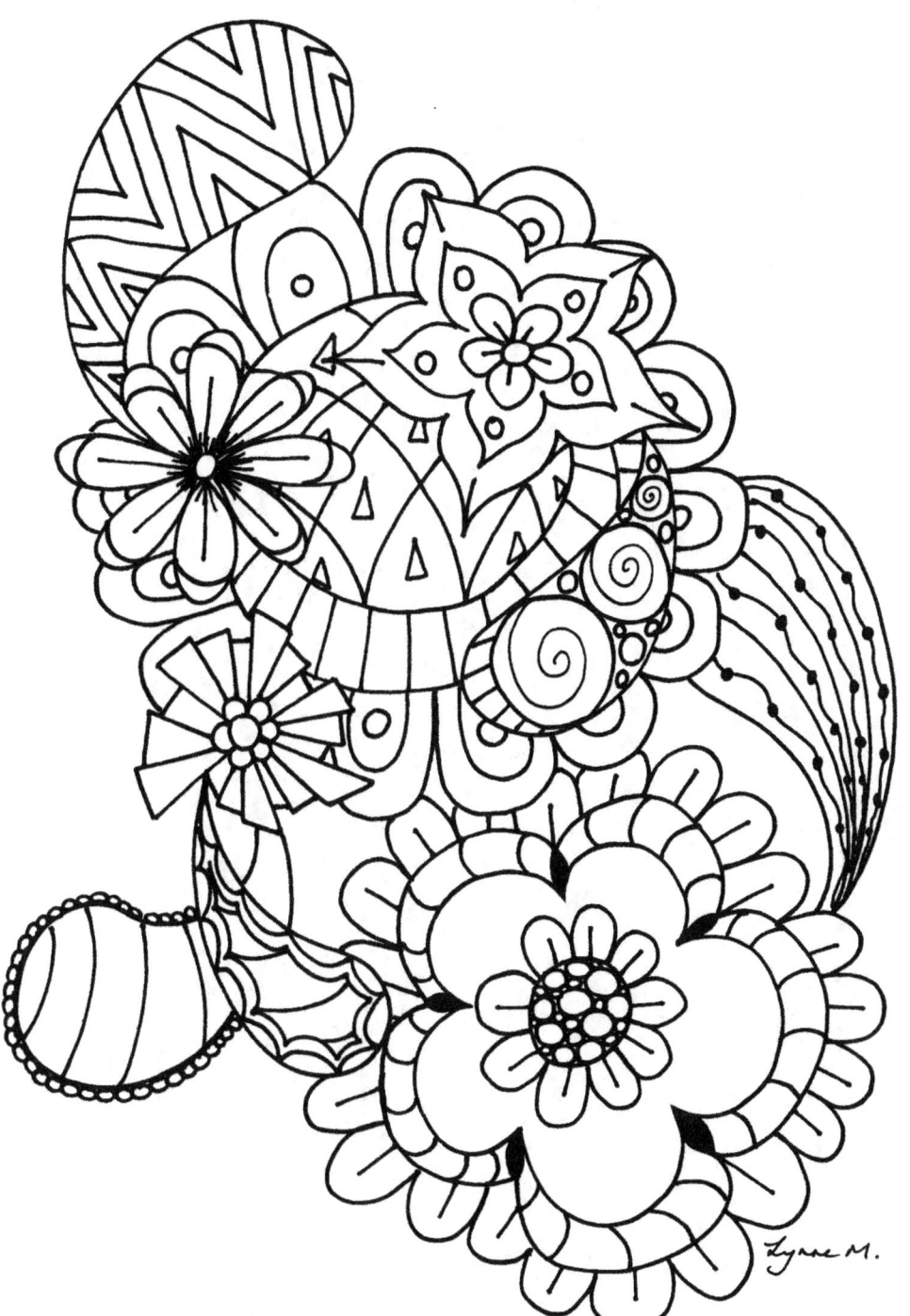

Contributing Artist
Lynne McGee
Brisbane, Australia

Facebook : Colorandtangle

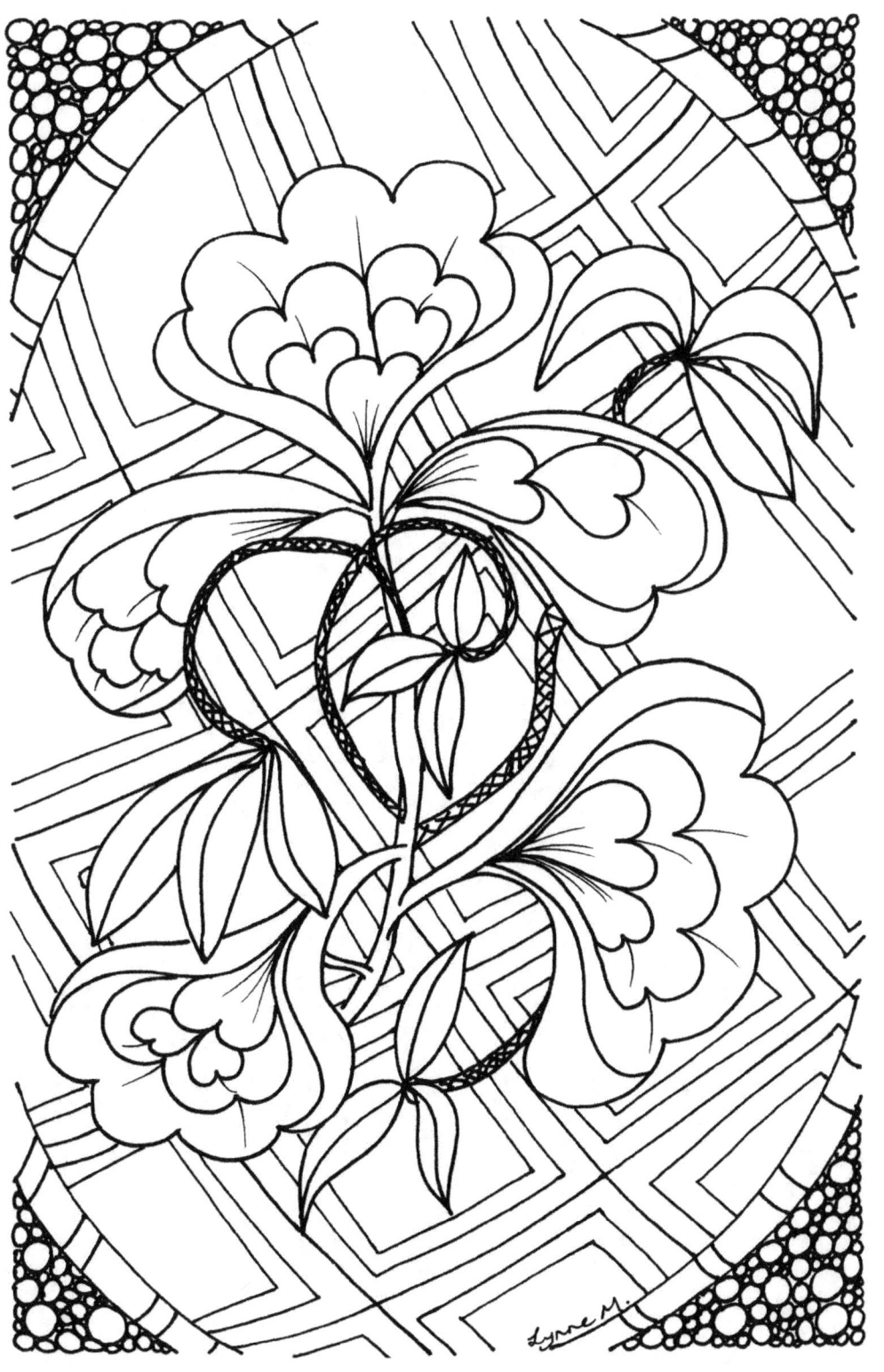

Contributing Artist
T.J.
USA

Facebook : TJsArtCorner

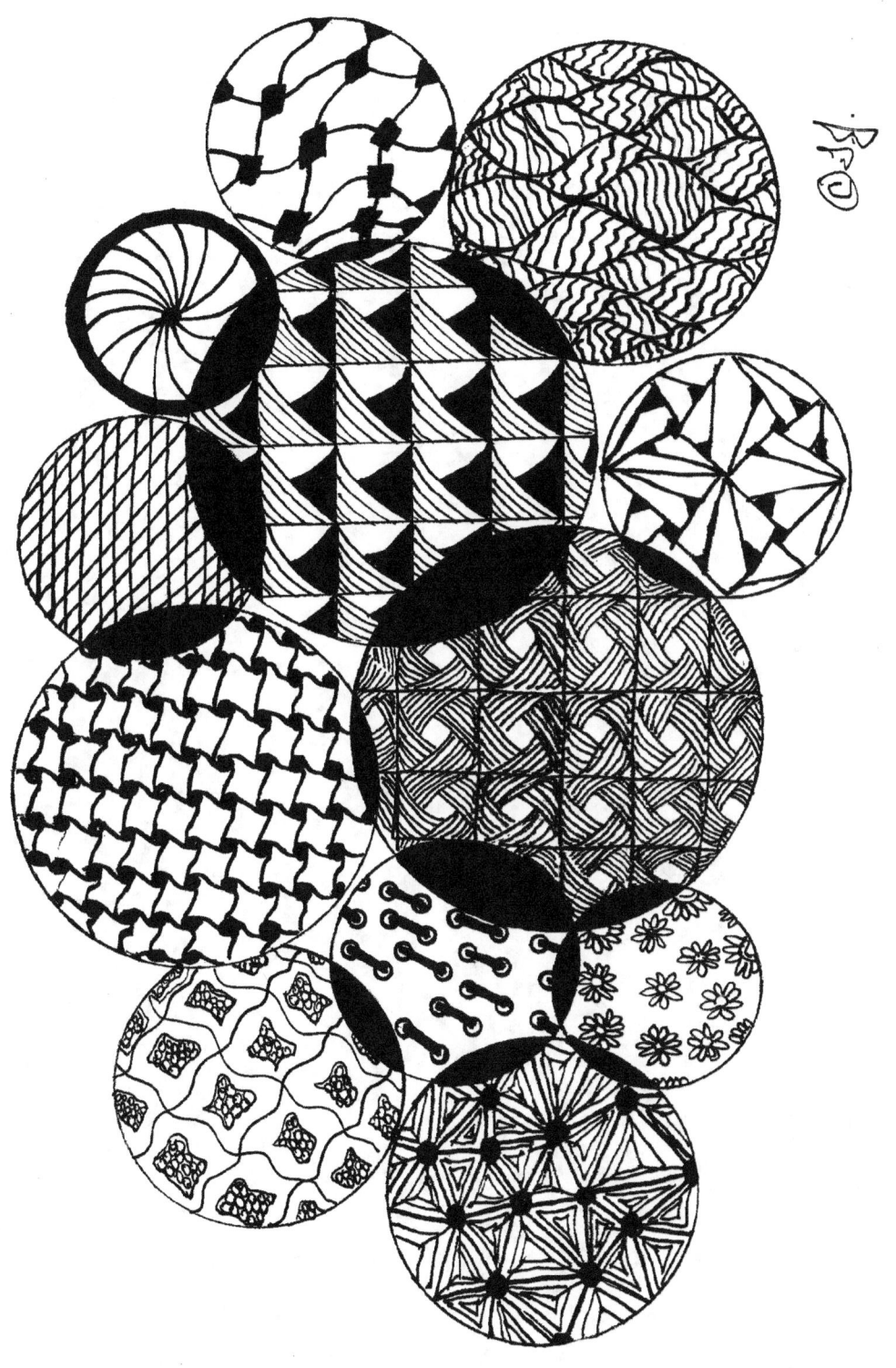

Contributing Artist
T.J.
USA

Facebook : TJsArtCorner

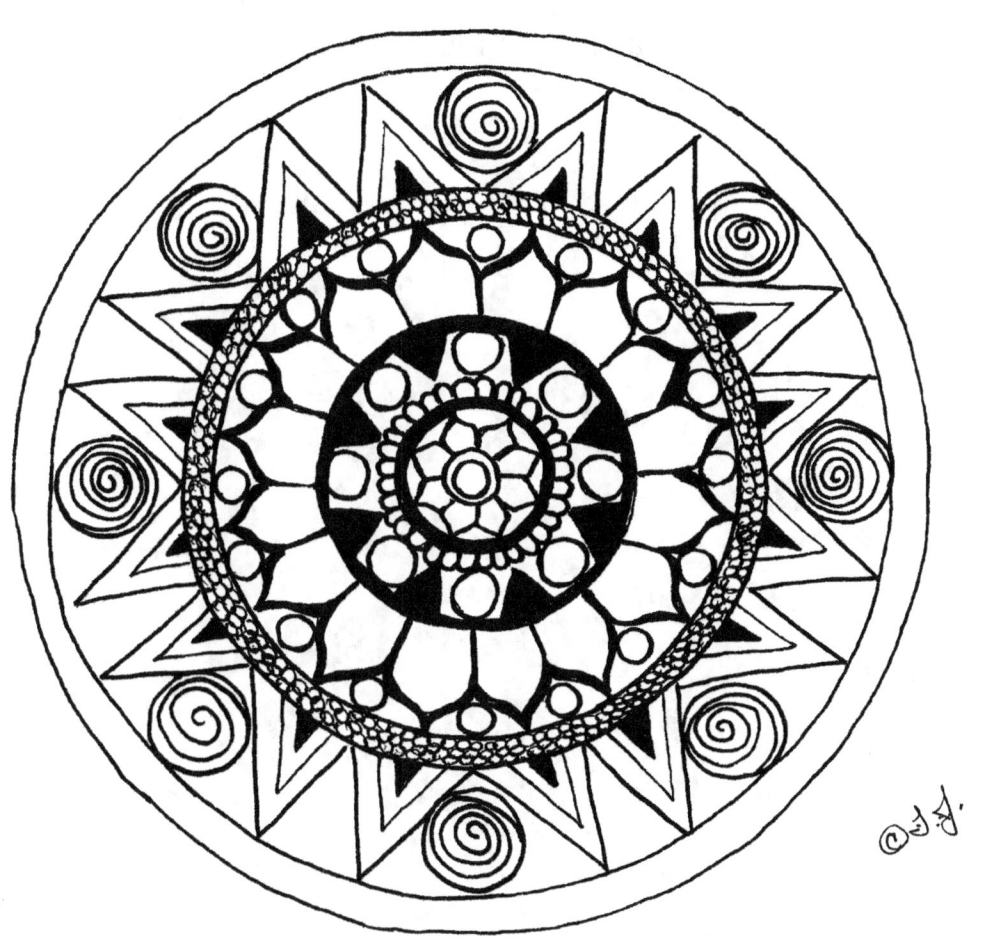

Contributing Artist
T.J.
USA

Facebook : TJsArtCorner

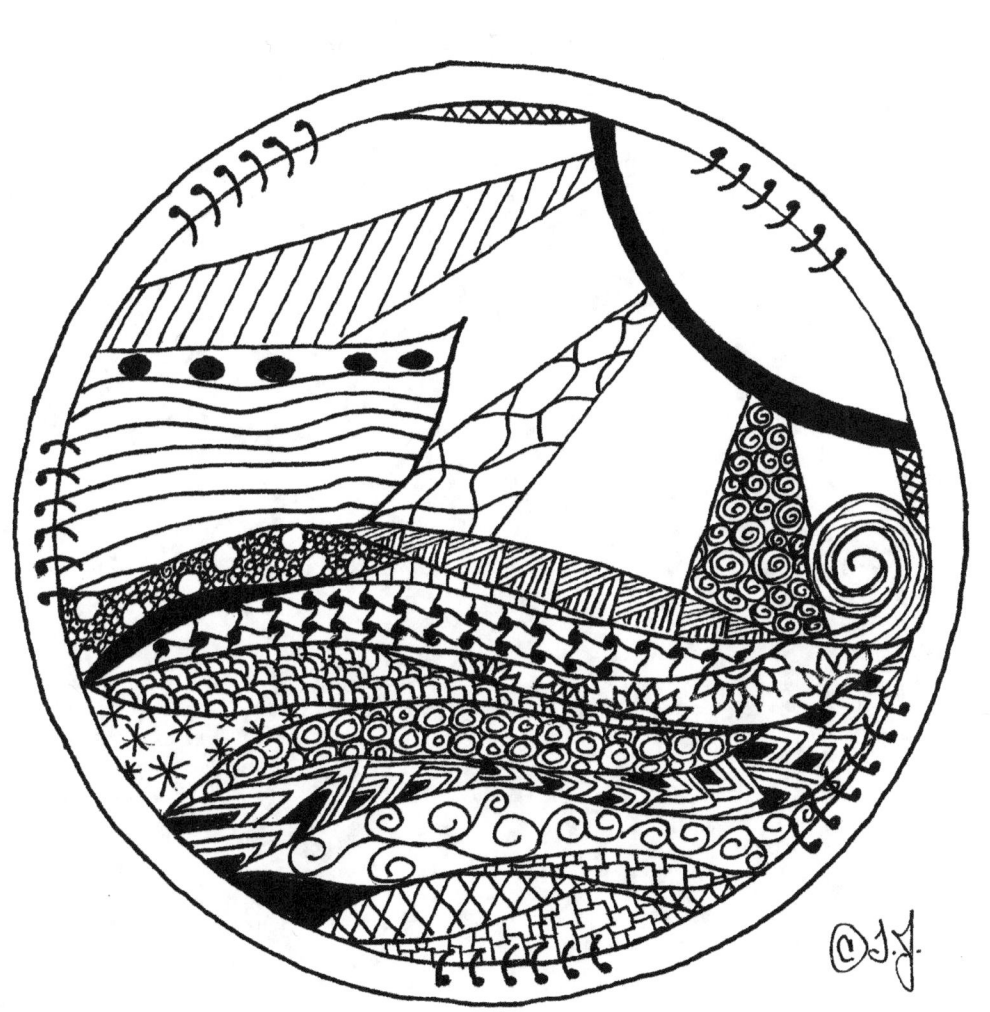

Contributing Artist
T.J.
USA

Facebook : TJsArtCorner

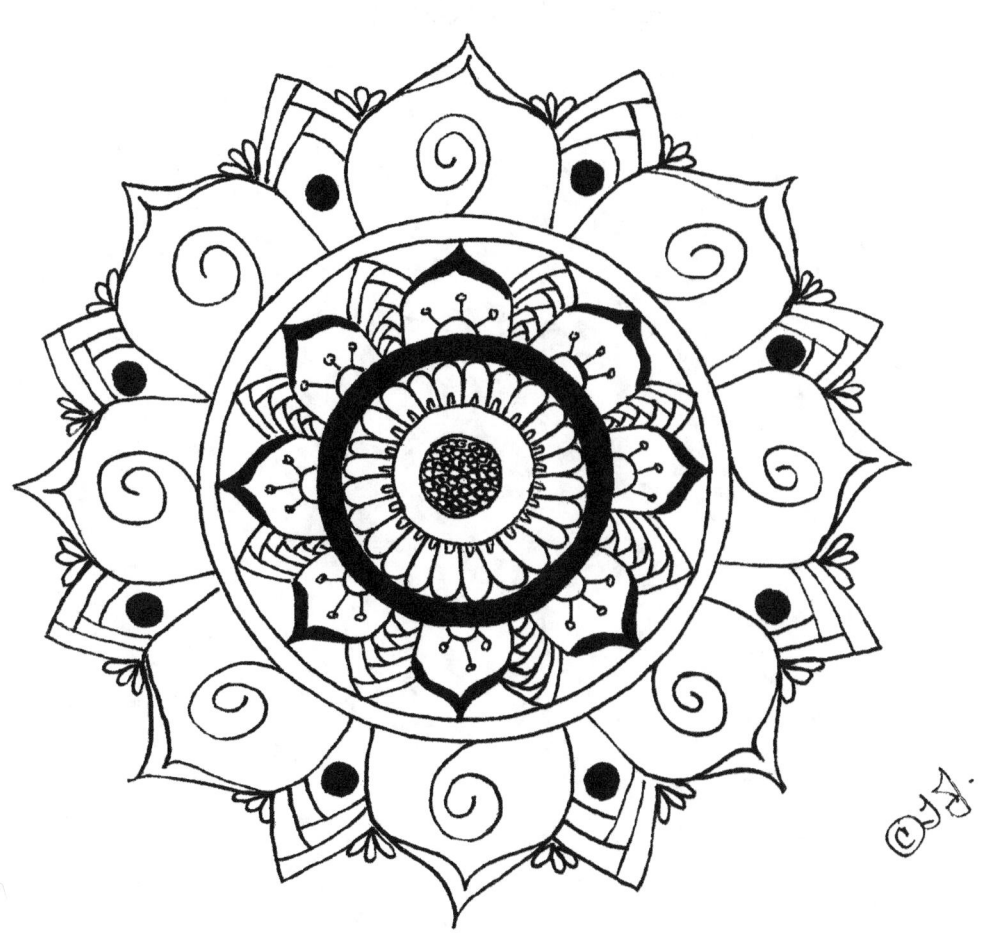

Contributing Artist
T.J.
USA

Facebook : TJsArtCorner

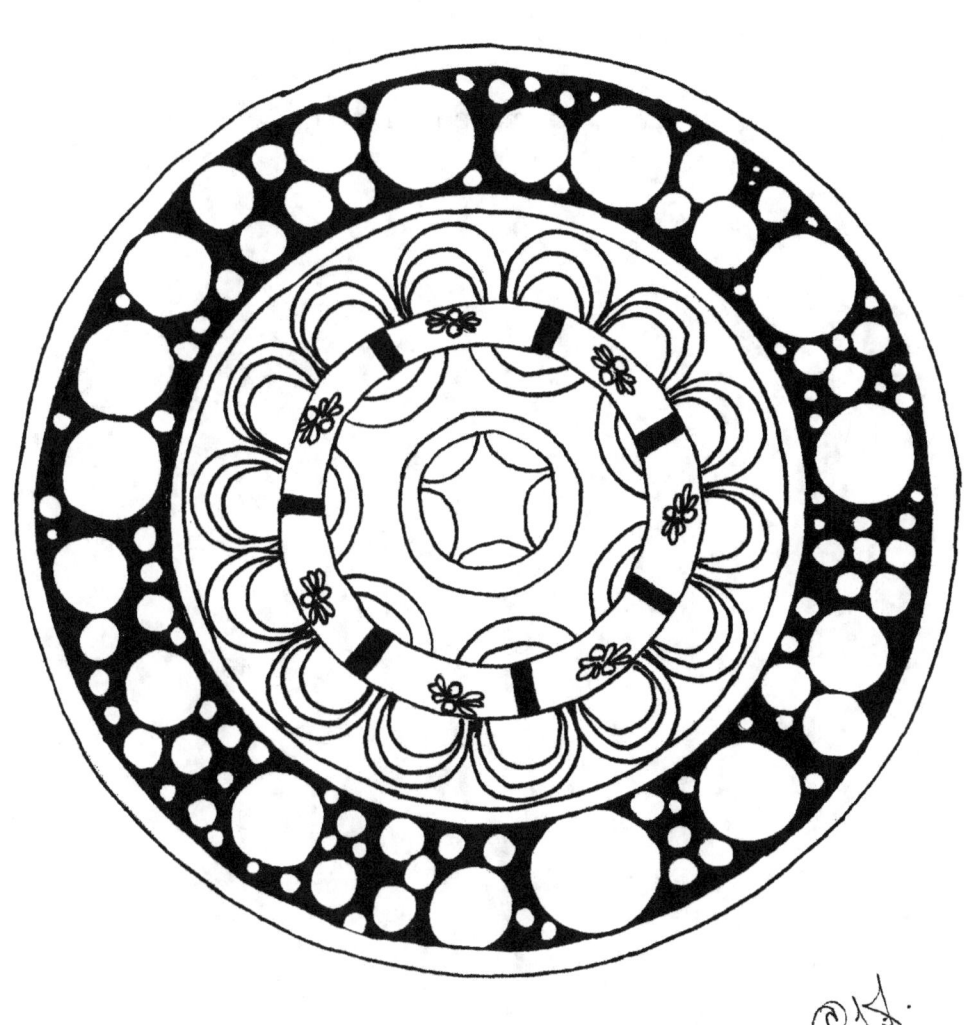

Contributing Artist
Marieke Raterman-Bos
Monnicken Werken
Monnickendam, the Netherlands

www.monnickenwerken.nl

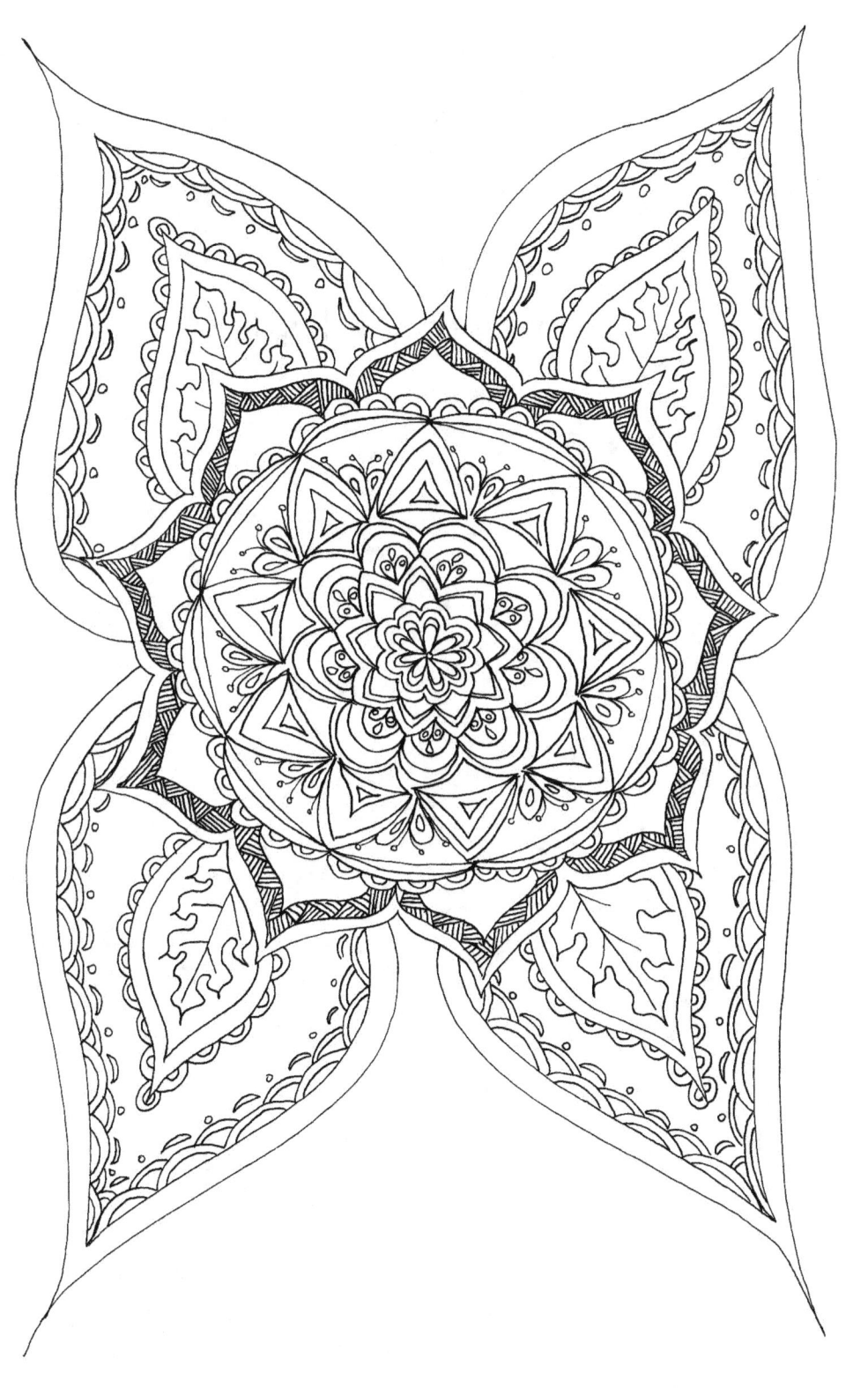

Contributing Artist
Marieke Raterman-Bos
Monnicken Werken
Monnickendam, the Netherlands

www.monnickenwerken.nl

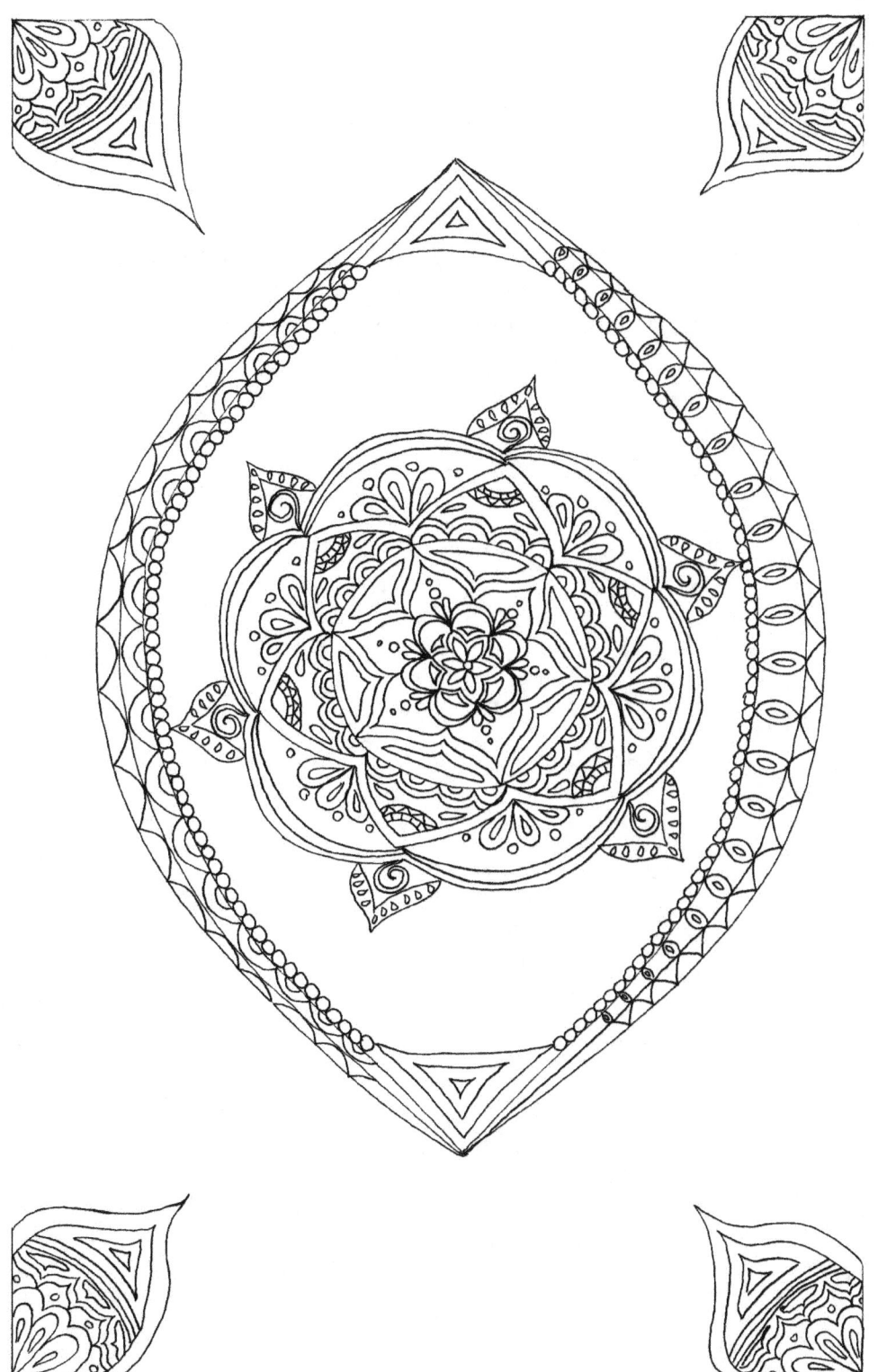

Contributing Artist
Ellen Wolters
The Netherlands

http://www.tekenpraktijkdeinnerlijkewereld.blogspot.nl/
http://ellenstraties.blogspot.nl/
https://www.youtube.com/user/DIWEllenWolters

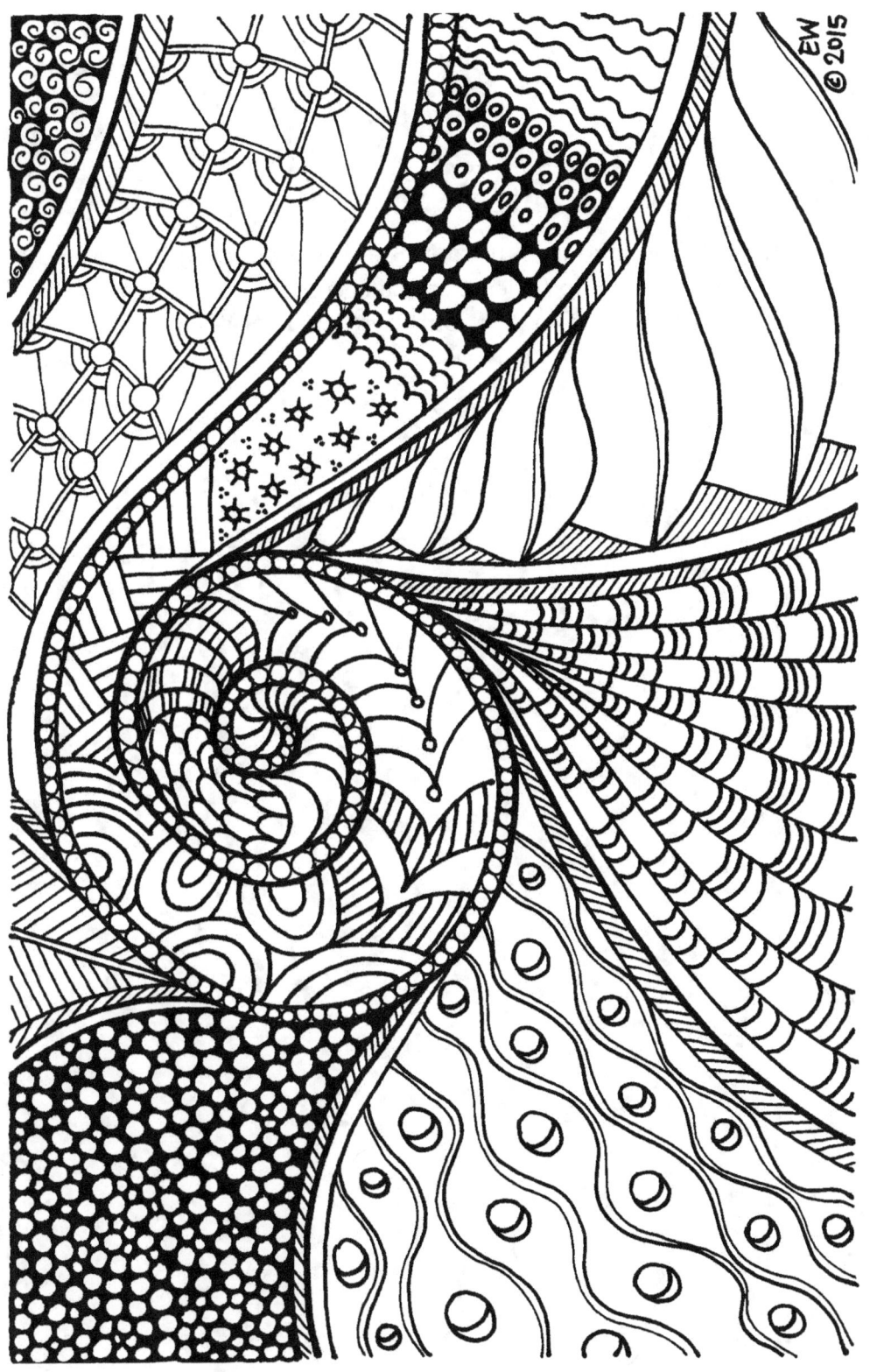

*Contributing Artist
Ellen Wolters
The Netherlands*

http://www.tekenpraktijkdeinnerlijkewereld.blogspot.nl/
http://ellenstraties.blogspot.nl/
https://www.youtube.com/user/DIWEllenWolters

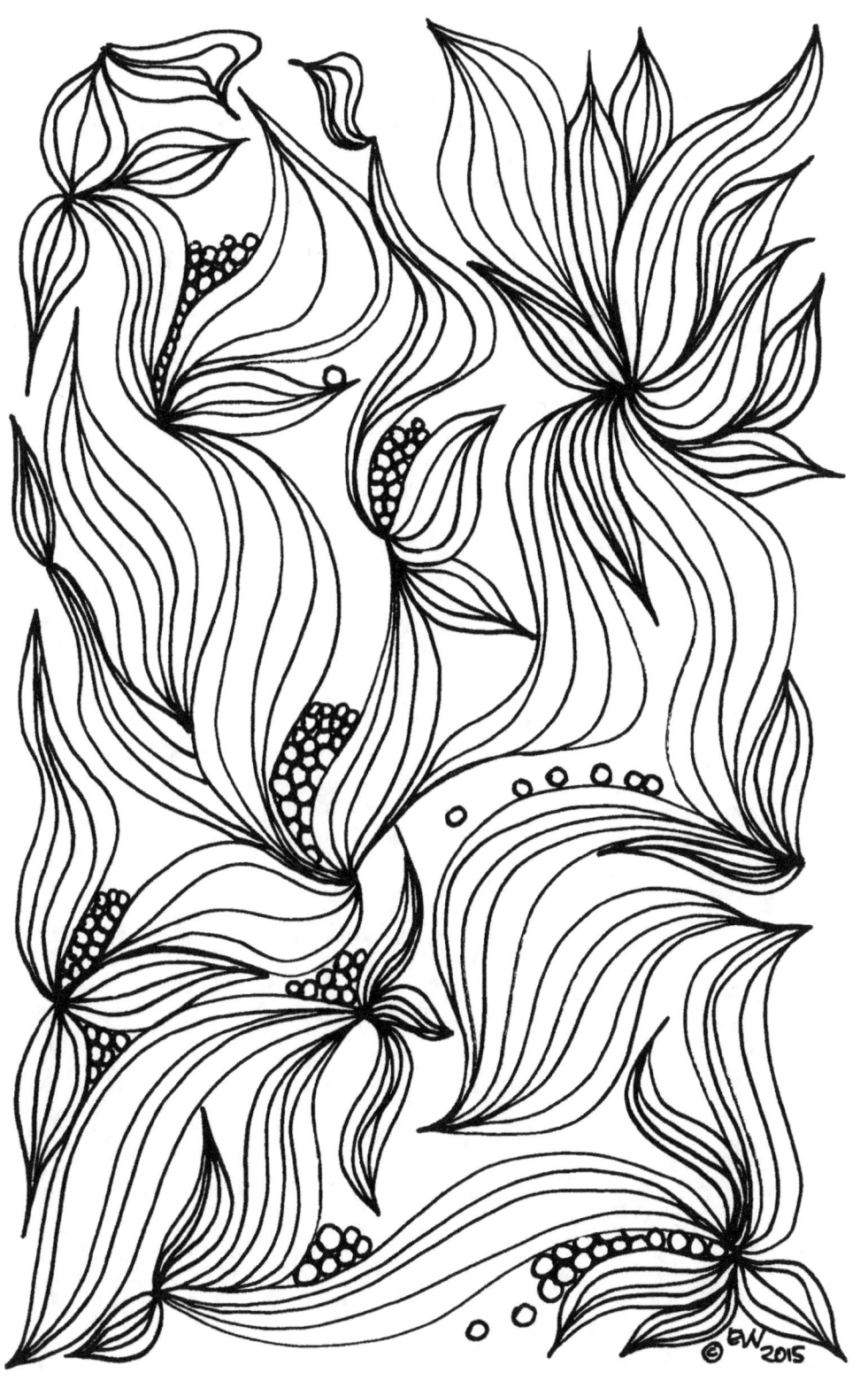

Contributing Artist
Mireille Westerduin, Colour by Mi
The Netherlands

Facebook : Colour-by-Mi-Kleurplaten-Illustraties

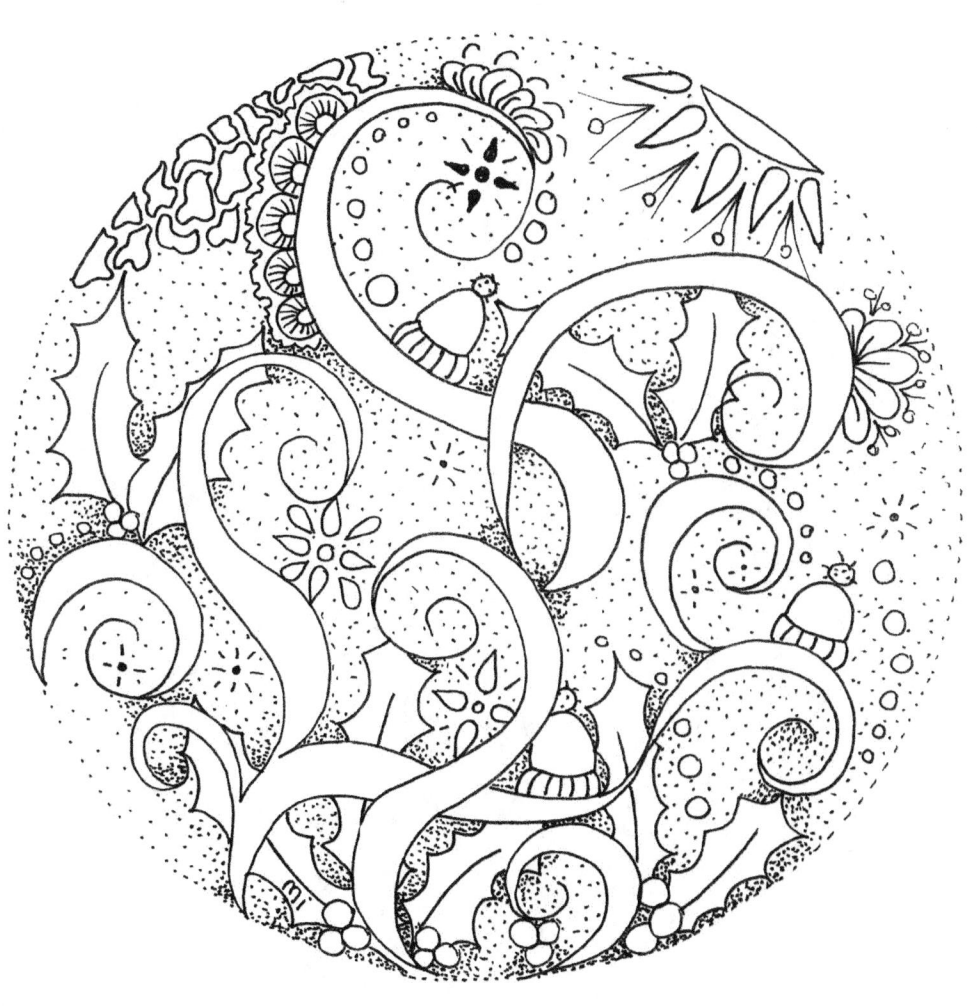

Contributing Artist
Mireille Westerduin, Colour by Mi
The Netherlands

Facebook : Colour-by-Mi-Kleurplaten-Illustraties

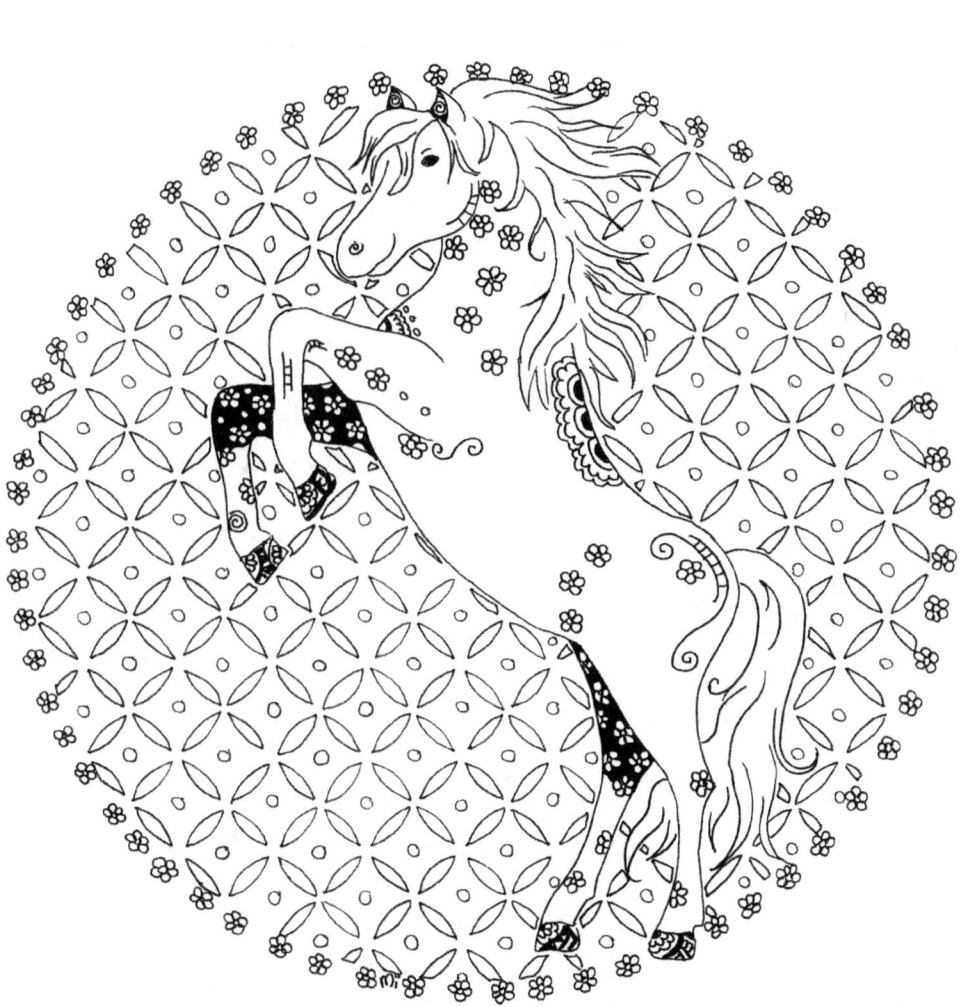

Contributing Artist
Mireille Westerduin, Colour by Mi
The Netherlands

Facebook : Colour-by-Mi-Kleurplaten-Illustraties

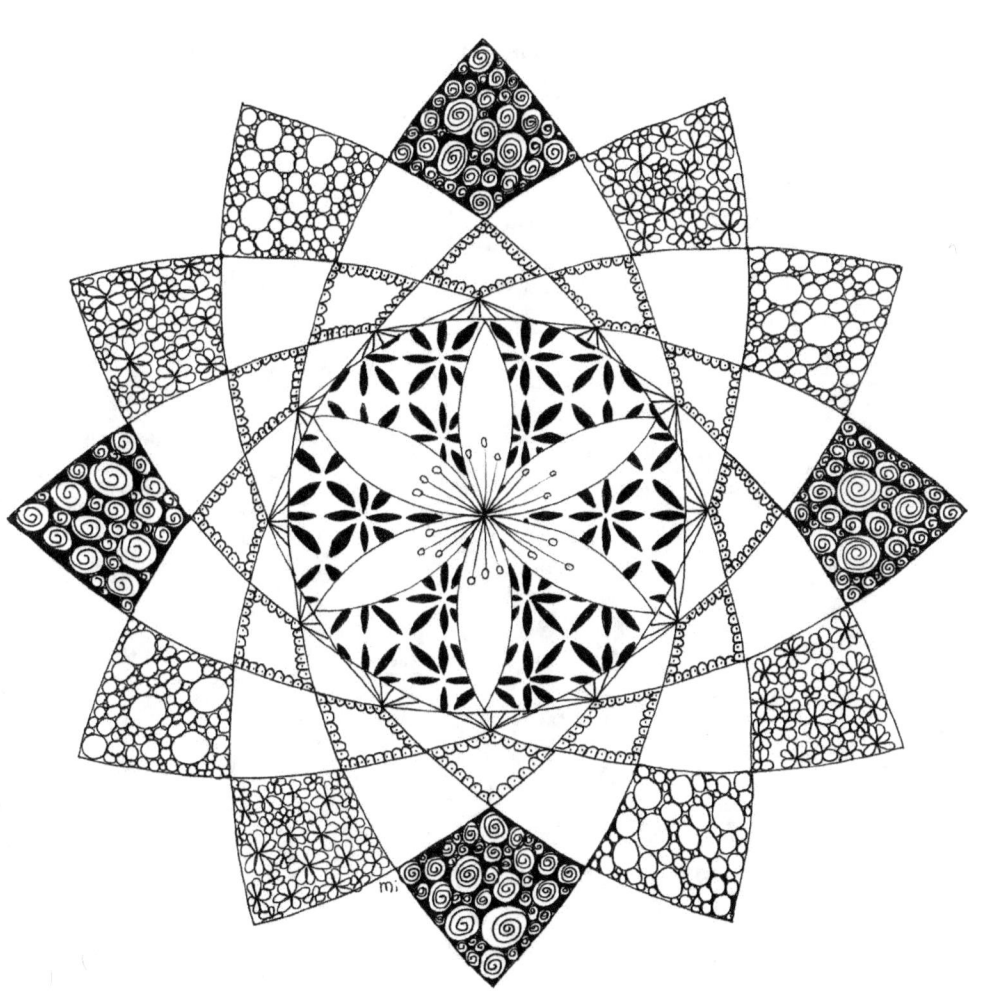

Contributing Artist
Nancy Liu
Taiwan

Facebook : 43Nancy43

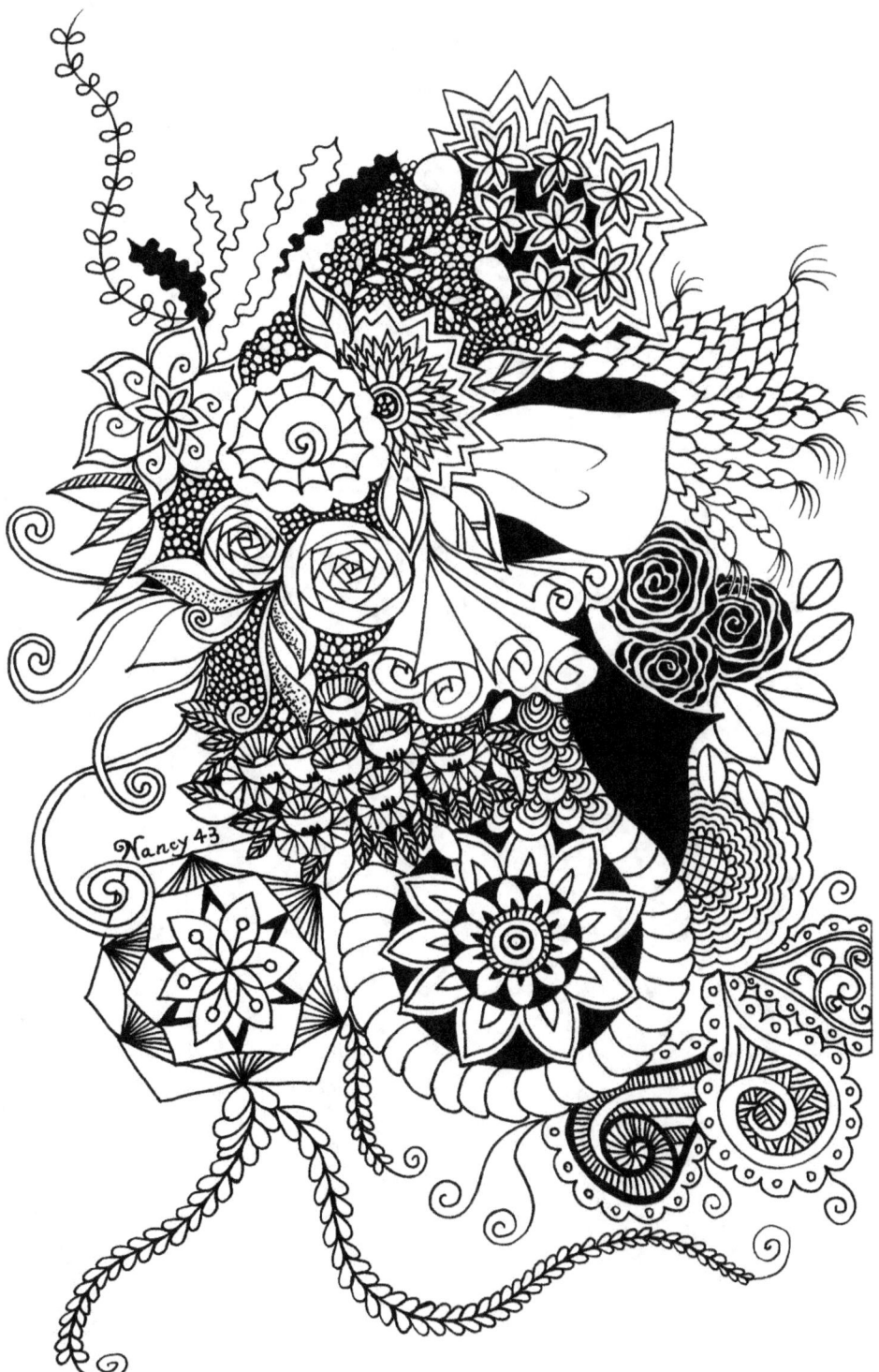

Contributing Artist
Nancy Liu
Taiwan

Facebook : 43Nancy43

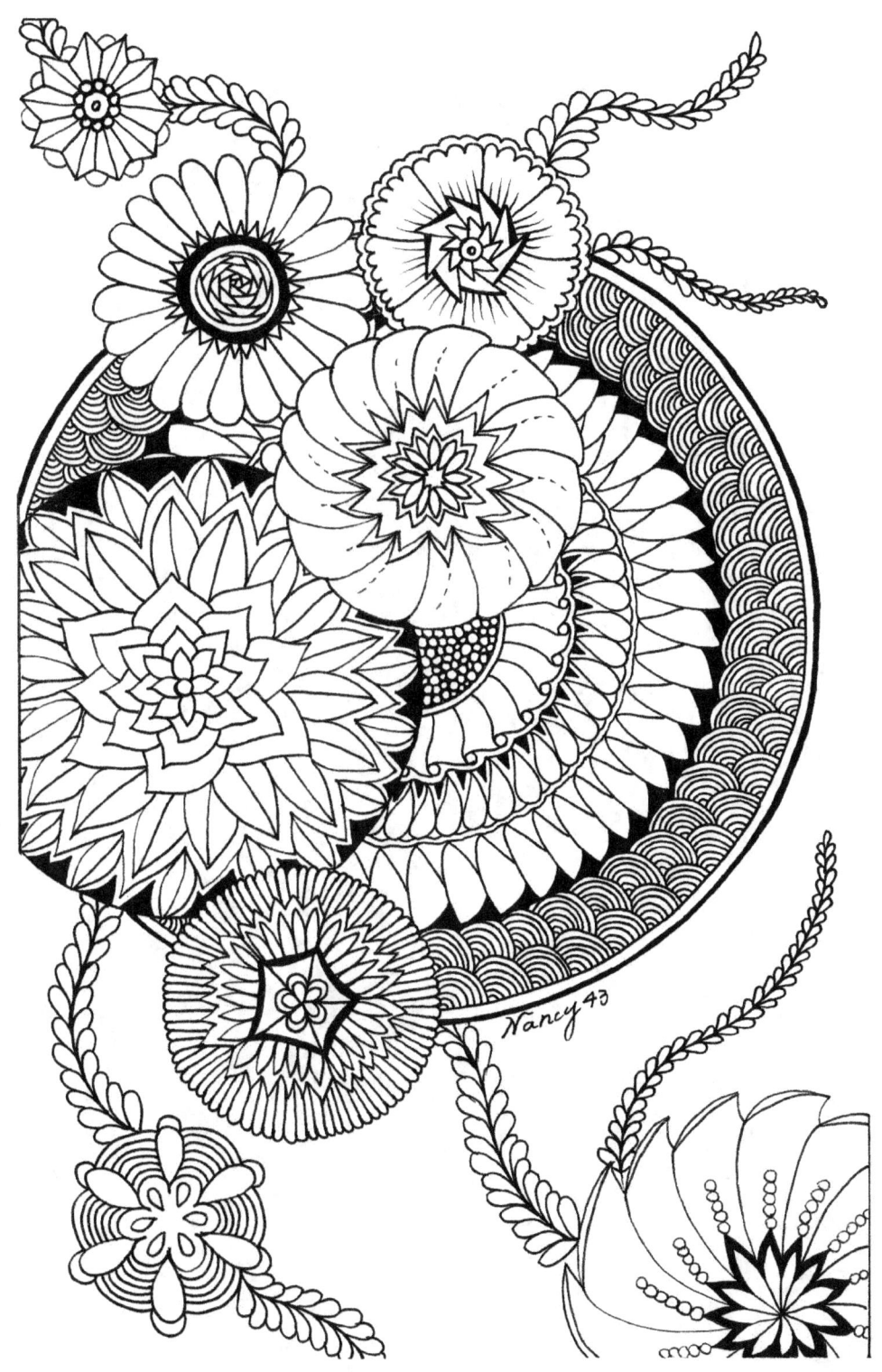

Contributing Artist
Peggy Sue's Artwork
The Netherlands

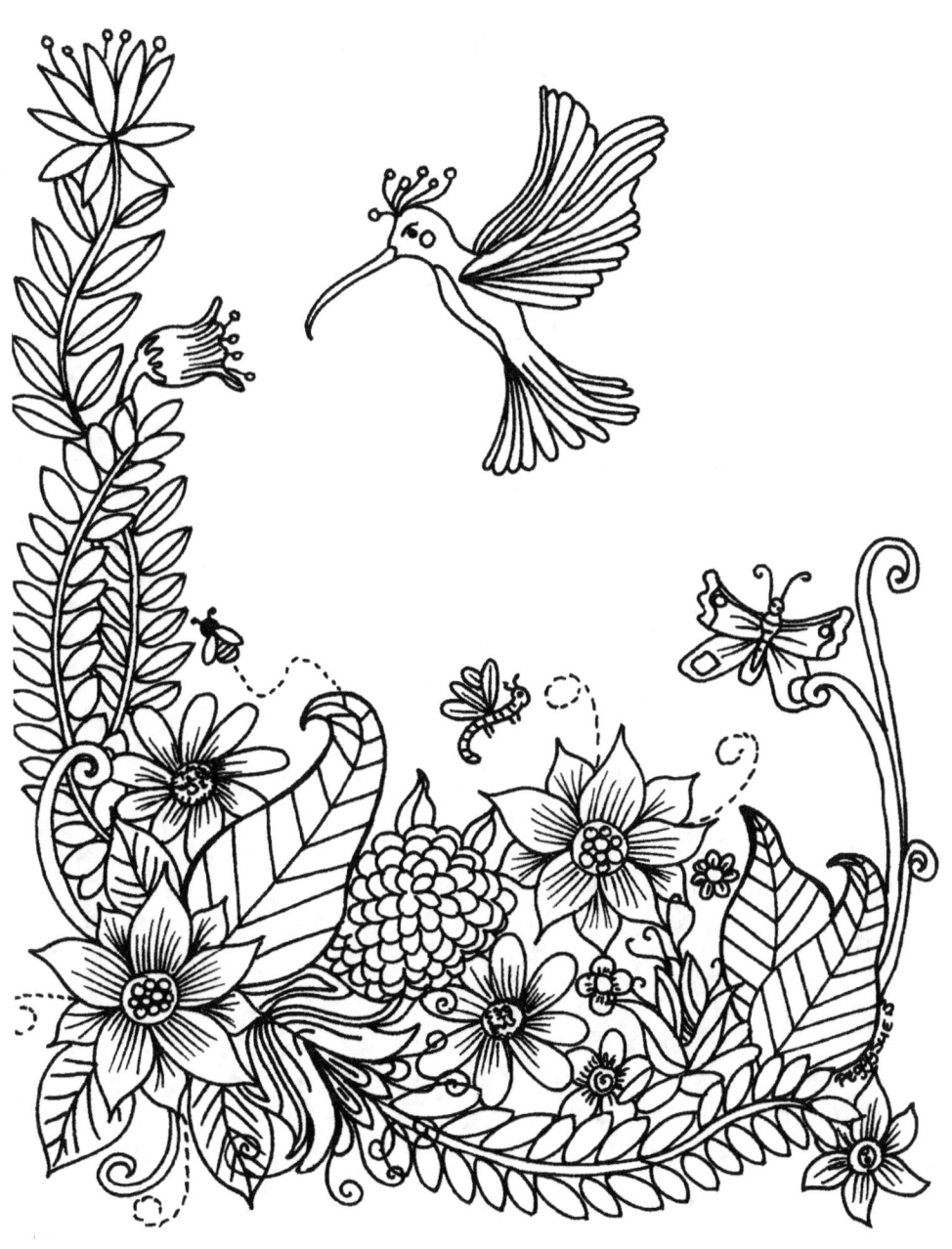

Contributing Artist
Peggy Sue's Artwork
The Netherlands

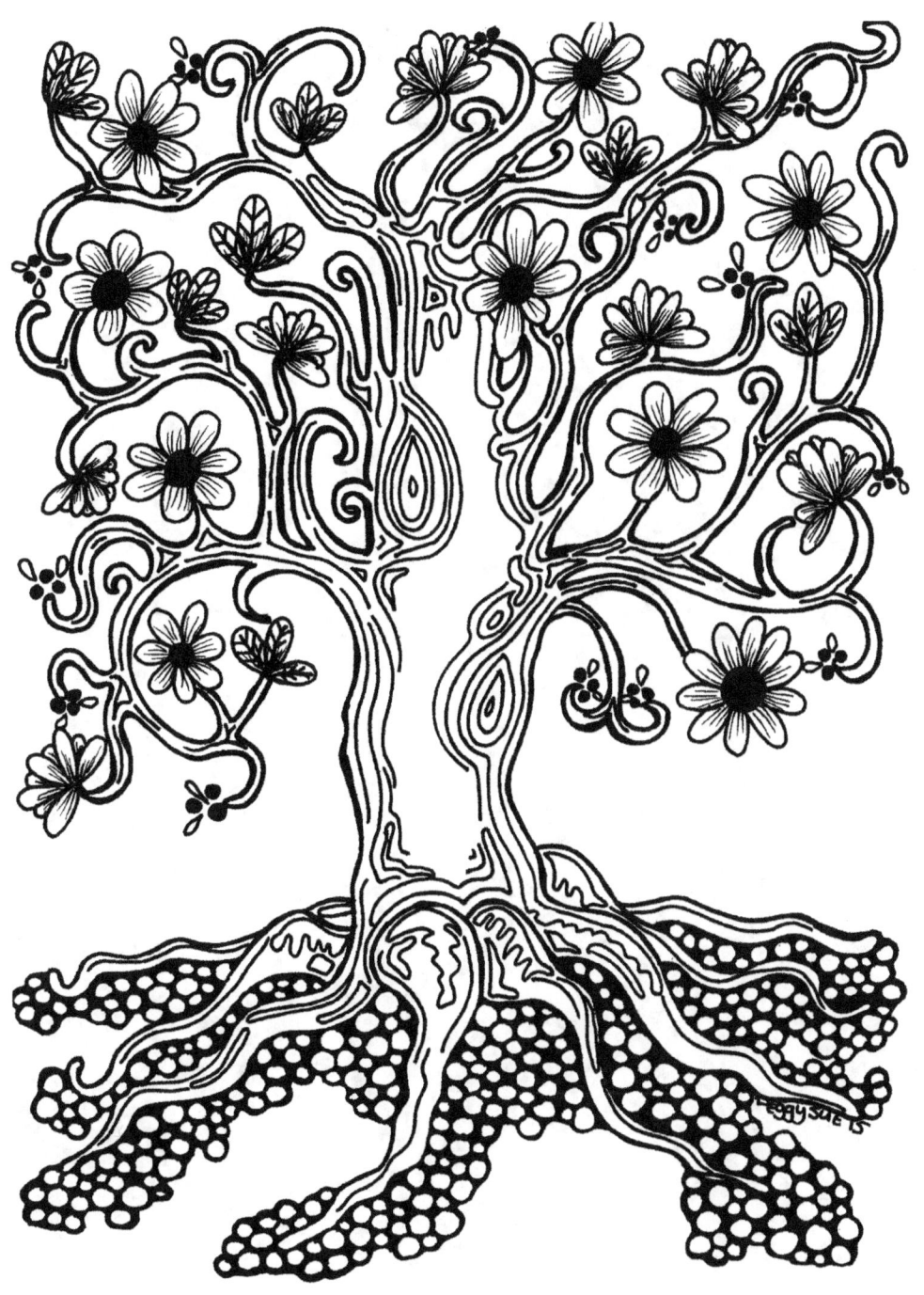

Contributing Artist
Peggy Sue's Artwork
The Netherlands

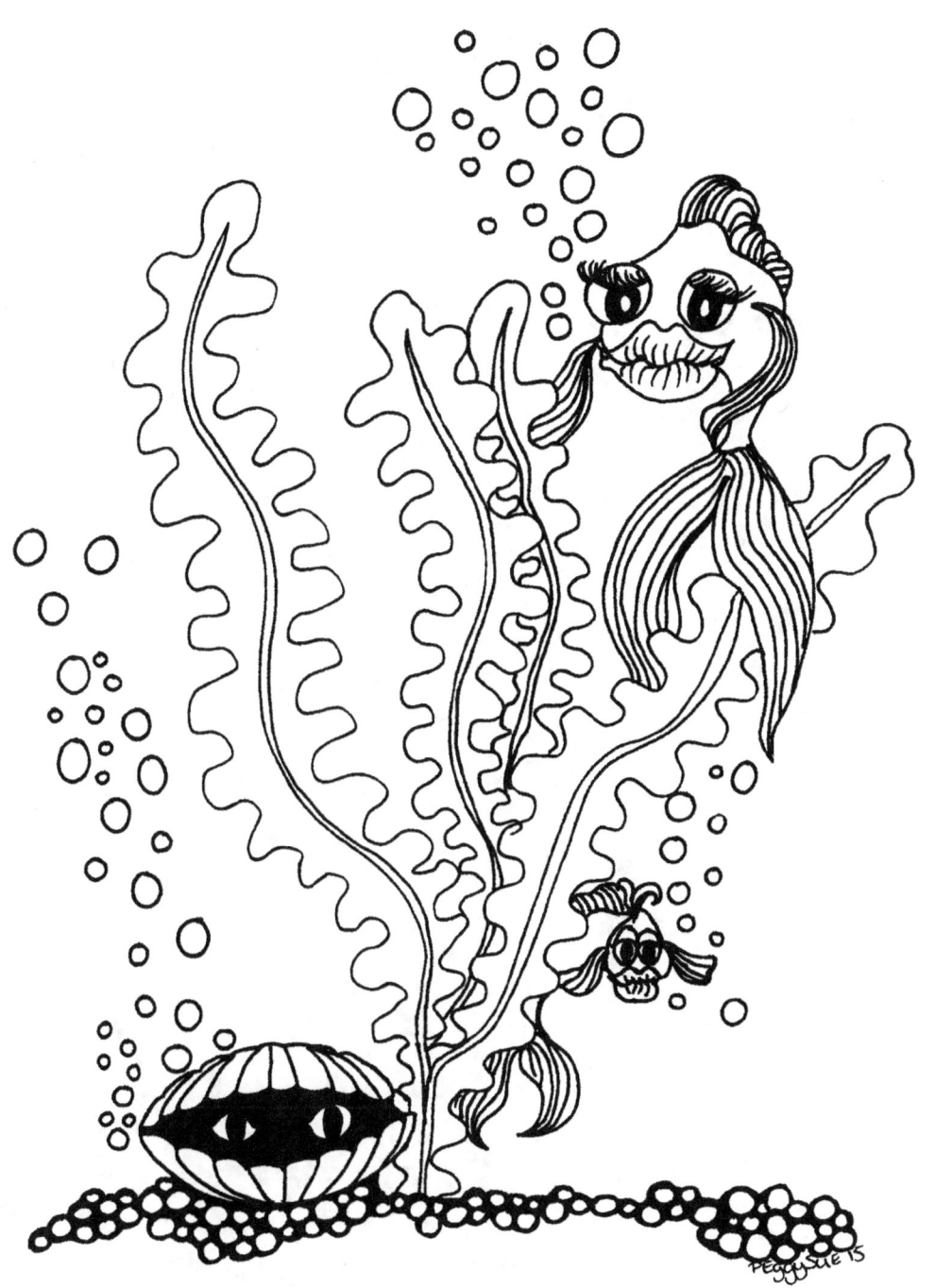

Contributing Artist
Peggy Sue's Artwork
The Netherlands

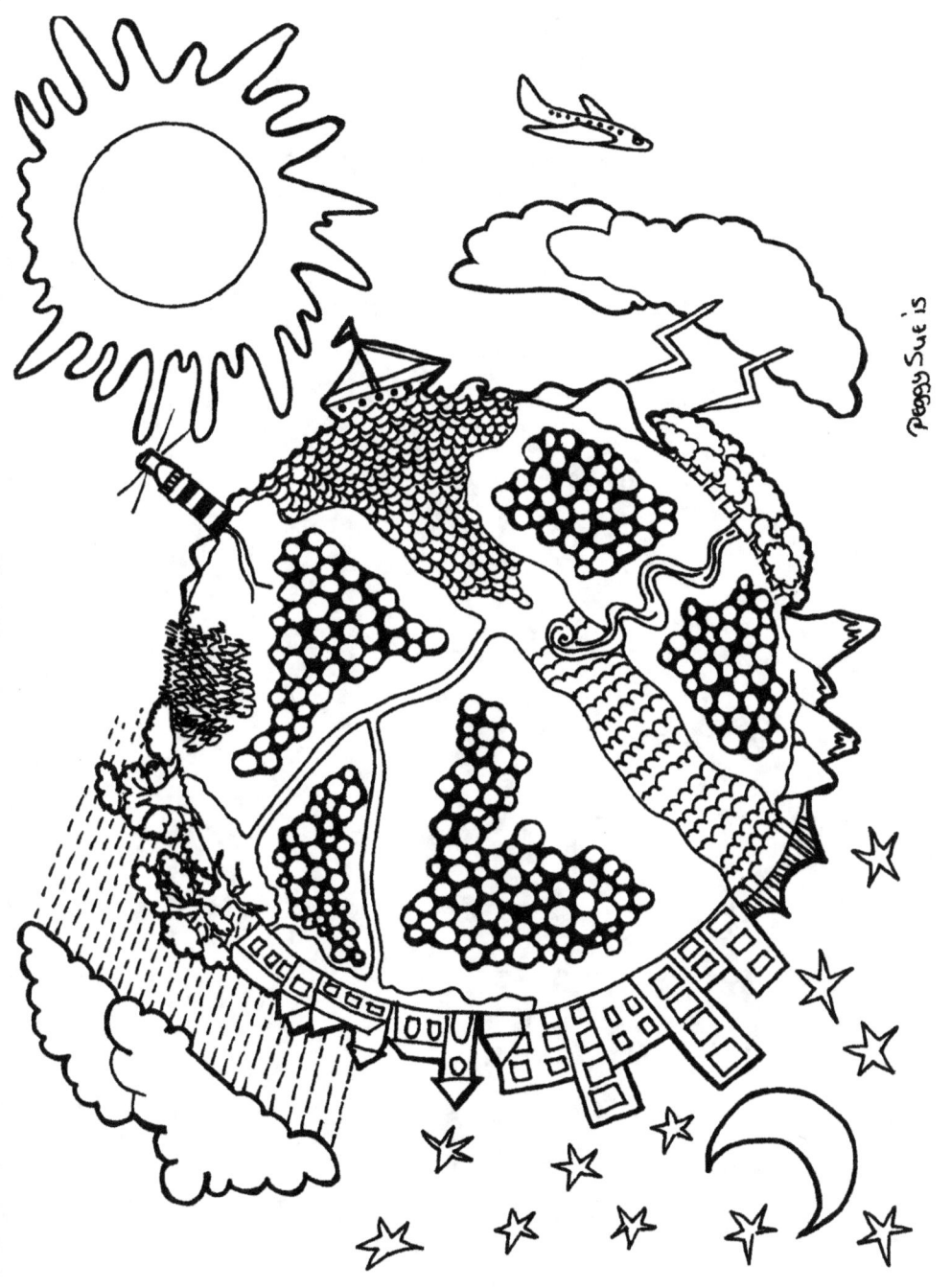

Contributing Artist
Rover Hsiao
Taiwan

Facebook : roverhsiao2015

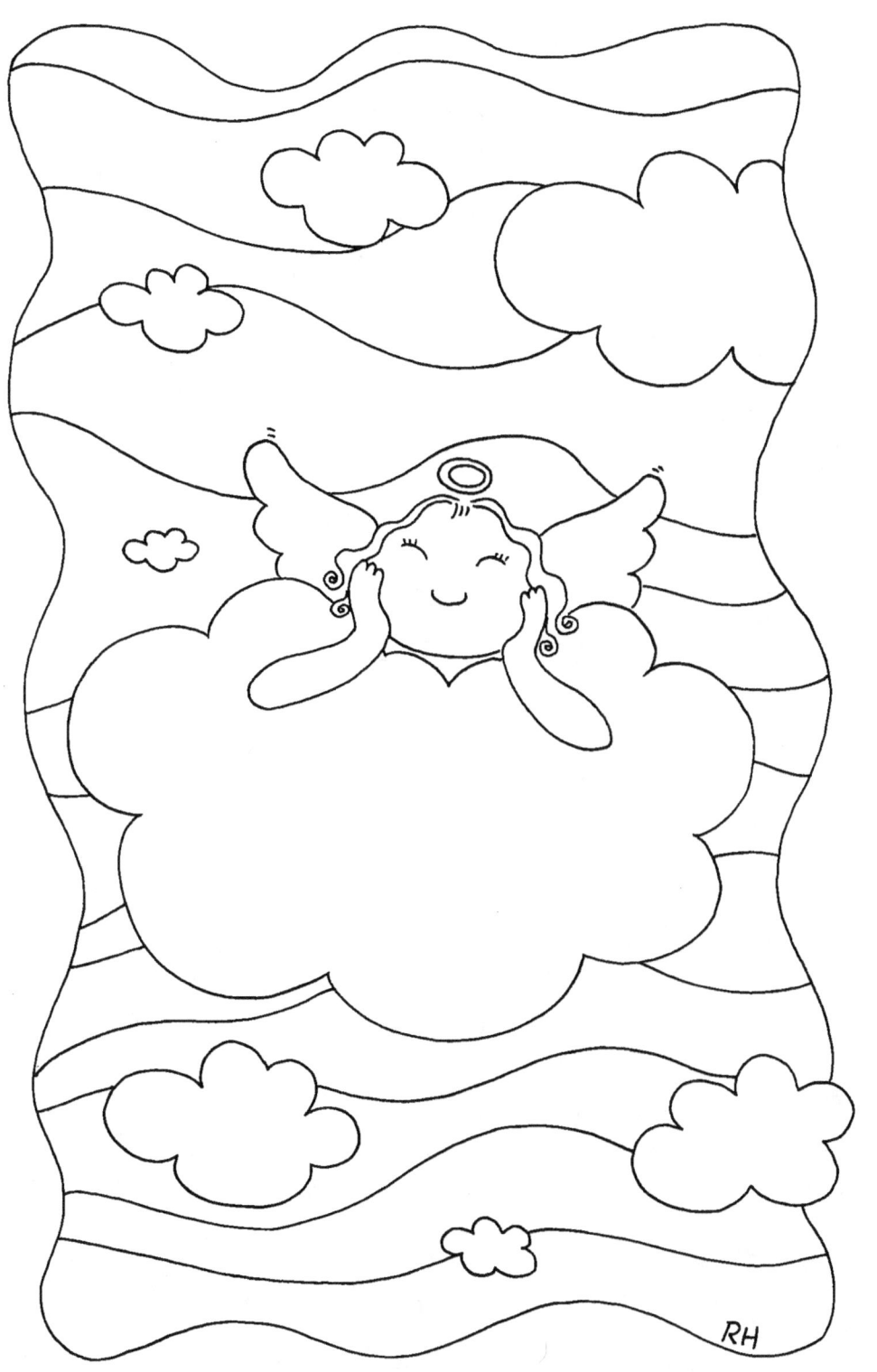

Contributing Artist
Rover Hsiao
Taiwan

Facebook : roverhsiao2015

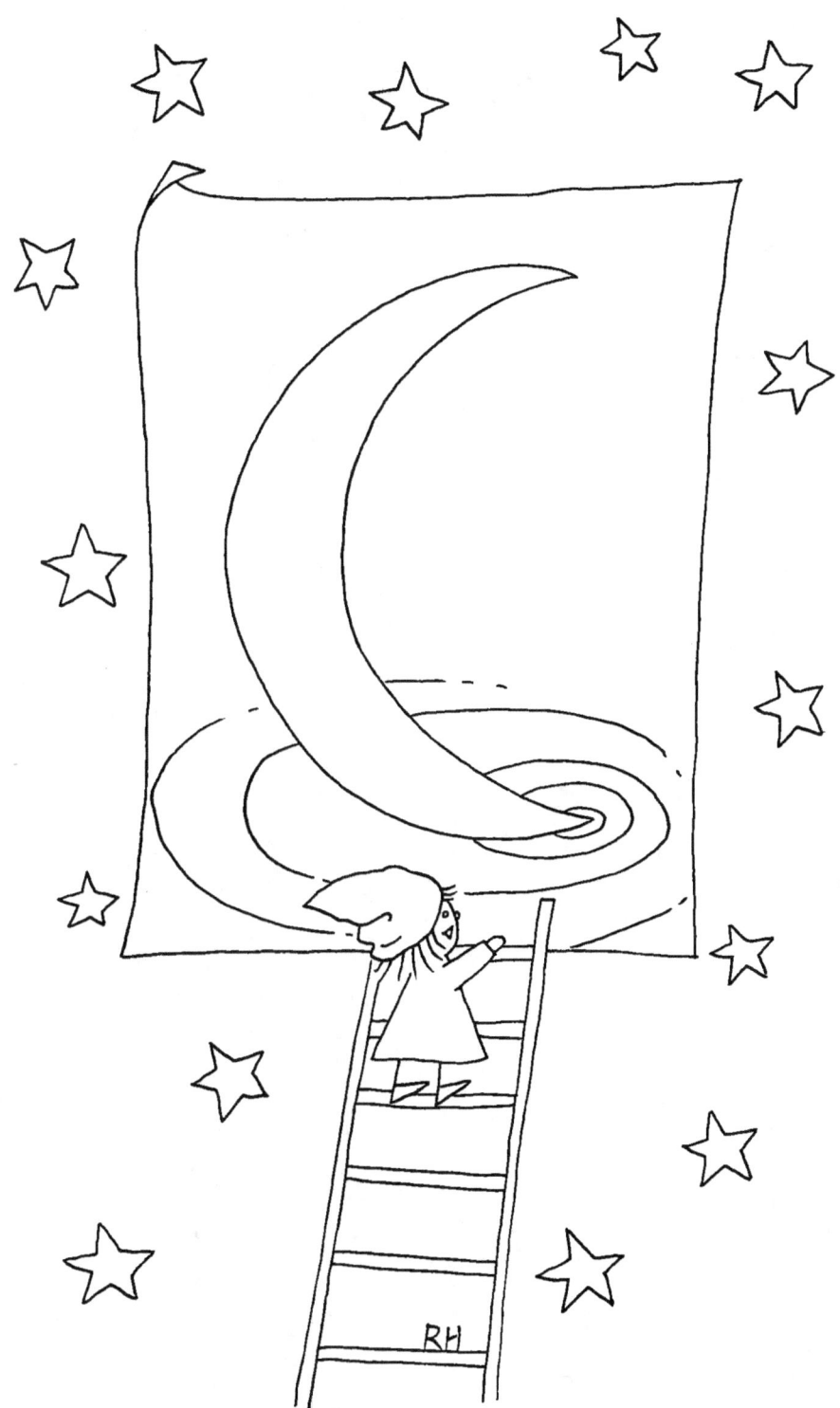

Contributing Artist
Velvet Comeau
Canada

Facebook : tranquilmoonart

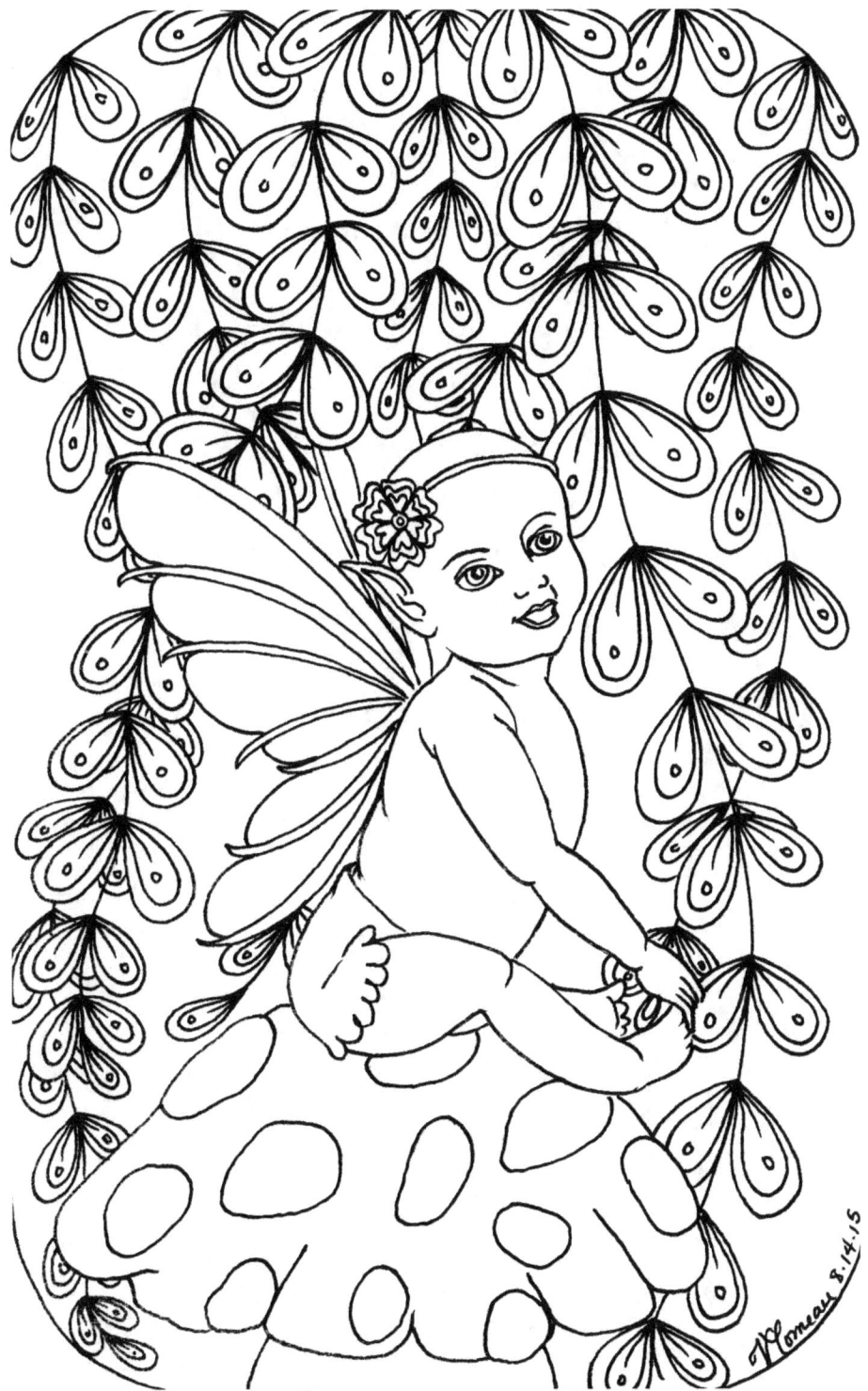

Contributing Artist
Velvet Comeau
Canada

Facebook : tranquilmoonart

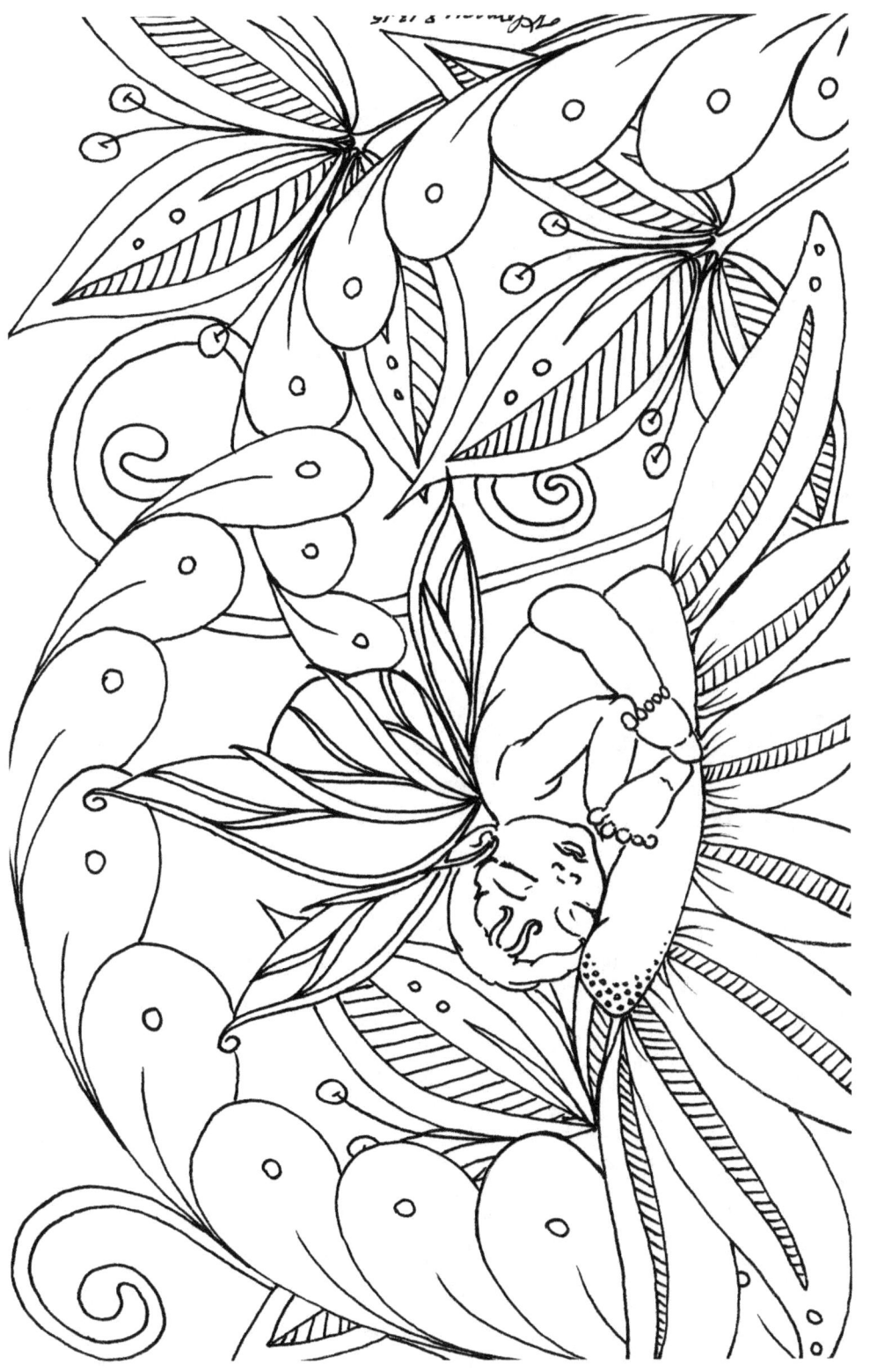

Contributing Artist
Velvet Comeau
Canada

Facebook : tranquilmoonart

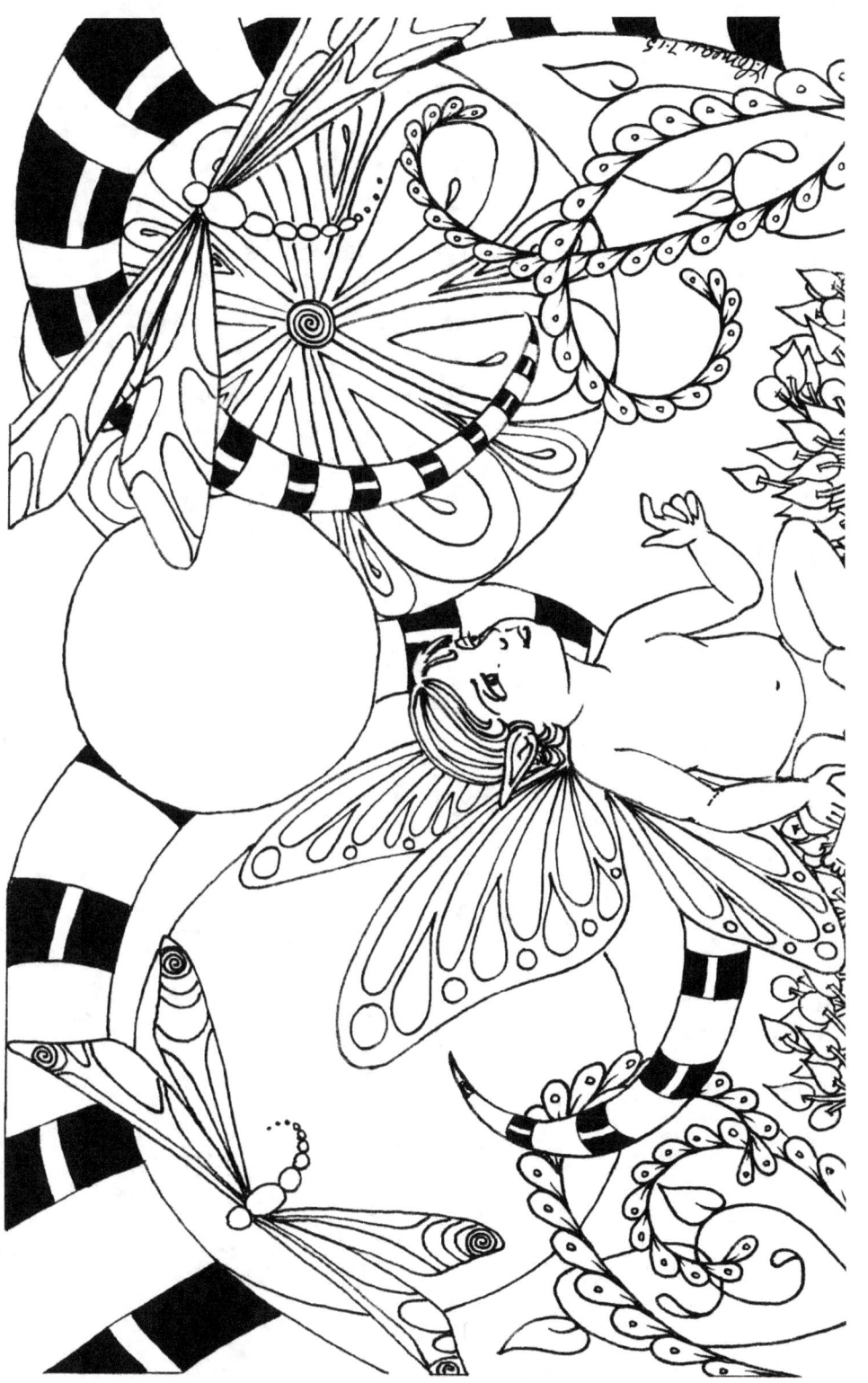

Contributing Artist
Diana Holmes
USA

Facebook : WhimsicalCheers

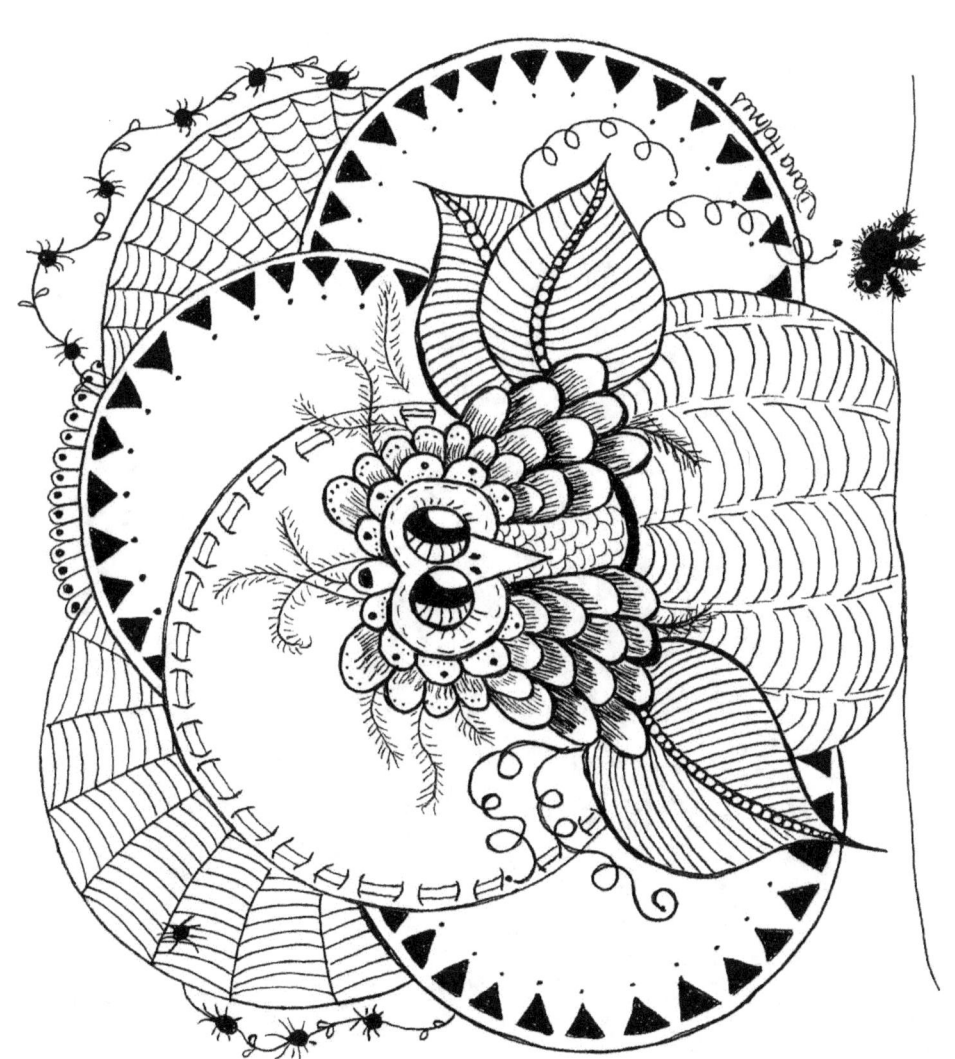

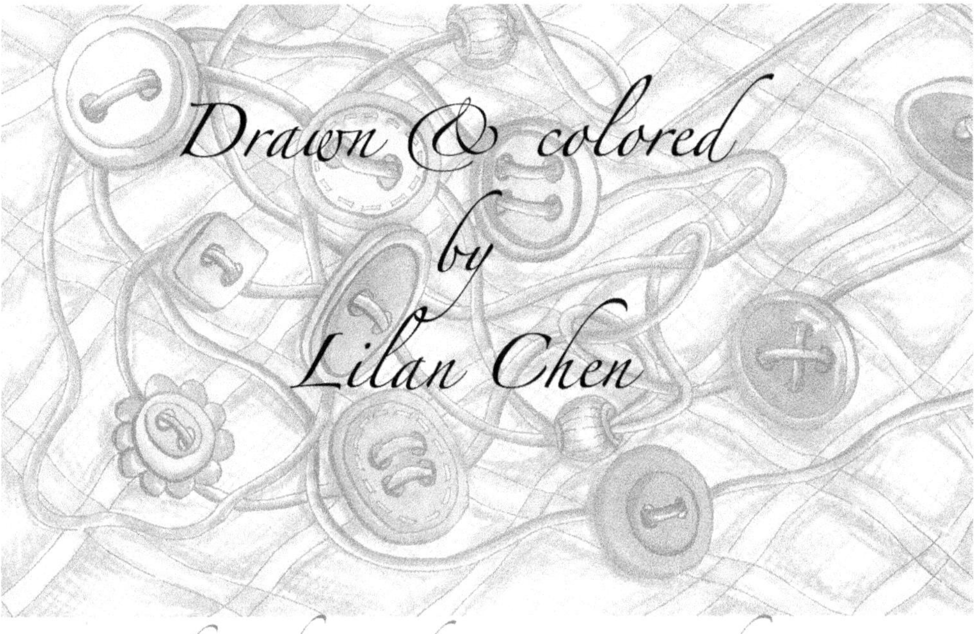

Drawn & colored by

Lilan Chen

Looking forward to presenting the next Mini Collection with 50 more designs!

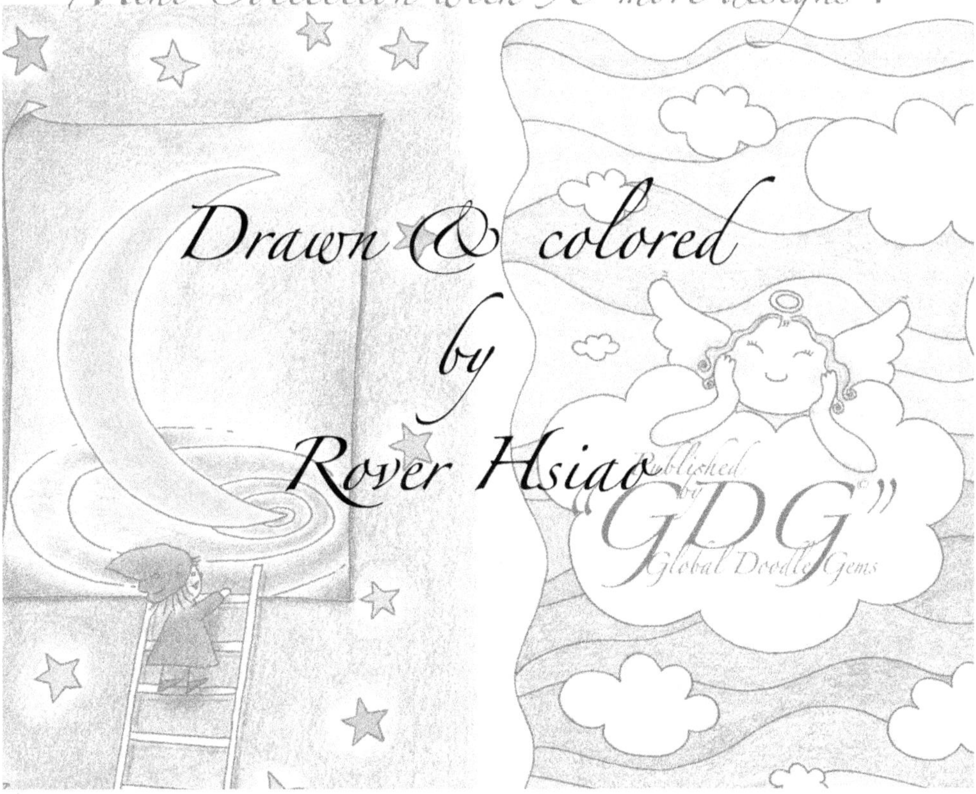

Drawn & colored by

Rover Hsiao

Published by "GDG"
Global Doodle Gems

www.ingramcontent.com/pod-product-compliance
Lightning Source LLC
Chambersburg PA
CBHW050116230526
45470CB00004B/1850